EDDIE MAY

...ory

...ddie May
...ary Wharton

'For Marlene, Harry and Joyce'

© **2012 Marlene Raybould**
All Rights Reserved
ISBN 978-0-9573497-0-4

Published by: Marlene Raybould
Design by: Emma Lamport www.emmalamport.com
Printed and bound by: Harris Printers, Porthcawl

Thanks to the Wrexham Leader, Wrexham FC, Cardiff City FC, South Wales
Echo and Southend United FC for permission to use their photographs/
programme covers. If any copyright of images has been inadvertently
breached, please contact the author so that it can be rectified for future
editions of the book.

Thankyou to Jeff White of Jeff White Motors whose support helped make this
book possible.

CONTENTS

FOREWORD

His time was up. But oh what a time! Bucket loads of laughter and almost equal amounts of tears, particularly over our last years together. Eddie arrived at Ty Gwyn Guest House, Cathedral Road twenty two years ago, cardiff City used my guest house for new players and coaching staff. A huge man with an even bigger suitcase, Eddie was hell-bent on causing as big an impact as possible. Morning One: when I brought his breakfast into the dining room, he looked at his plate and said, "Have you dropped some?" Life was to continue with Eddie in a similar vein. If there was any more to be had, he was up for it!

Eddie was a giant of a man, a real charmer, an amazing character. It was evident even then that this man was a powerhouse, capable of managing men, charismatic and uncompromising. Focused and single-minded, he went for what he wanted and invariably got it. Eddie always left an impression on the people he met. He was a people person and everyone loved him. He was a character and also a very complex man.

During those years at Ty Gwyn, if fun was to be had, we were there. We had an amazing time, living a life full of laughter. Eddie grew to love my Dad and Mum, Harry and Joyce, treating them with enormous respect. He was full of admiration for Emma and Harriet, my daughters, amazed at their creativity and freedom of spirit, referring to them always as his daughters. Eddie often accompanied Harriet when she sang in clubs around Wales, even setting up a music agency together when football work dried up.

Sixteen years ago while Eddie was working in Torquay, Harriet gave birth to a baby girl, Elizabeth Emma, known now to us as Libby, "beautiful Libby". The United Chairman came up to Eddie to tell him Harriet had given birth. He offered his Rolls Royce to rush us back to Cardiff. Eddie cradled Harriet's little girl - the rest is history. Bampy was born. He was smitten. His outpouring of love for Libby knew no bounds: unconditional love. Their relationship has been one of total joy and love for one another. Every holiday, every spare minute, we spent with Libby, our happiness and laughter became louder and more meaningful.

During this time, Eddie's dear Mum died. He was devastated. He loved his Mum so much. Stories were told of Eddie's Jewish Orthodox Grandfather and his mother, Miriam, and his Dad, Joseph. I saw another side of this complex man: compassionate Eddie. With all this in mind we went to Bethlehem and Jerusalem so that he could explore his heritage.

Eddie placed his message in the wailing wall and we lit a candle in the church in memory of his Mum - a truly spiritual experience for both him and me.

We travelled extensively - Africa, Norway, Finland , Egypt - the list goes on. Shipwrecked in Norway, confronted Black Mamba in Africa, offered a farm from the Minister of Culture in Mugabe's government, Ground 0 at Victoria Falls , Climbed the Motopos mountains to find cave paintings. So many stories, many in this book. What an amazing life! I think we have laughed our way around half the world.

And then disaster struck over eleven years ago.

Eddie had heart failure and nearly died. Eddie refused to accept that he had had more than a little setback. Times were quite difficult with Ed refusing to accept that he would have to take things easy, his medication was vital and a change of lifestyle unavoidable. All alcohol consumption stopped. He began to eat more healthily. His medication appeared to be controlling his symptoms. Things looked good but his life expectancy was not great.

Family matters were amazing and we were to experience even more happiness in 2006 when Bebe was born, Emma and Jason's little miracle. Eddie once again became a doting Bampy pushing the pram with great pride. When the girls stayed over, they would ring a bell for "room service". Eddie would go to them with treats on a tray: biscuits, ham sandwiches, hot chocolate, etc. He was to them a wonderful, funny, idiotic, caring and very loving Bampy. Silly hats on his head, rolled up trousers, card tricks, magic and very very bad jokes. Not Eddie May, the footballer, just plain and simple "Dear Bampy". When Bebe was told that Bampy had died she said, "Nan, it will be all right. He was a Superhero. He told me."

How do you replace all this? He was a caring man with depths that took twenty two years to recognise. Every day he would express his love. His great concern was that he would not live long enough to see his precious Libby achieve all she wished for. His death was not unexpected. Days before he told me what a happy man he was. His death was a truly peaceful one. He was a very very happy man, sitting in his favourite chair, cup of coffee nearby, Tele on, in the home he loved so much.

Well, Eddie, we all love you passionately, unconditionally. I thank you for all those wonderful years. We loved, we laughed, and ultimately, he died. But in such a wonderful world we had a truly wonderful life.

Marl

As a Wrexham player, where I played a total of 334 games across eight seasons from 1968 through to 1976.

INTRODUCTION AND ACKNOWLEDGEMENTS

Working with Eddie during the course of this project has made me realise what an amazing career that he has experienced and sometimes, endured, in football. Across more than 50 years; from his early days playing as a striker in the Essex amateur leagues, to turning 'pro' in the 1960s and making a name for himself in the heart of the Wrexham defence of the 1970s and much, much more. Eddie was also at Swansea City when John Toshack arrived and he was in at the start of the club's amazing rise up through the divisions. As a manager and coach he has also seen some good times and not so great times; the pinnacle of his success coming when he led Cardiff City to a League championship and Welsh Cup 'double' in the 1992/93 season. It was whilst with the Bluebirds that the "Eddie May's Barmy Army" chant originated and he remains well thought of amongst the supporters there today who still sing the chant.

But that forms just a part of his unique story and I have been impressed by Eddie's ability to recall people and events from many years ago which he has shared with me during the compilation of this book. There have been far too many countries and clubs that he has been involved with as a player, coach and manager to list them here and so I would agree with a sports reporter who termed him "The Phileas Fogg of football". Like that intrepid explorer, Eddie's own travels have taken him to numerous places and so the title of his autobiography is apt. What comes shining through is his ultimate belief in being professional in both manner and approach, a belief that he has sustained throughout his career even under tremendous strain. He is a likeable person when you meet him, and chatting with him, you really get a feel of his life journey incorporating many professional, and personal, highs and lows. Speaking with some of his former colleagues, one of them being Paul Ramsey, Ed's captain at Cardiff City during the double winning triumph, said to him, "Are they going to be able to print it!" The answer to that is a positive one and I hope that you enjoy reading it as much as I have in relating it.

A big thank you to the big man himself and Marl for providing the foreword. Also to all the fans who have taken the time to share their own memories of Eddie with me. Many of you loaned photographs and related-items that proved very useful and your enthusiasm was appreciated.

Gary Wharton

Top: As a youngster with Southview FC in the 1960/61 season.
I'm in the front row, far right.
Thanks to team mate Arthur Smith, pictured behind me, for the photo.

Above: Life as a professional footballer with Southend United in 1966.
I'm pictured in the back row, first on the left.

1
THE BIG BOY FROM EPPING

I was born Edwin Charles May in Epping, a small market town and leafy suburb in Essex on 19th May 1943. Our family lived in West Ham, a district south west of there which by 1965 would be incorporated into London. My father, Joseph, or 'Joe' as he was known, worked at the world famous Smithfield meat market, where upon leaving school in 1958, aged fifteen, I joined him. Living in West Ham, as you can imagine, the 'Hammers' soon became our favourite team and it was where my interest in football blossomed. He would take me to all the home games at their Upton Park ground, often having to put me on his shoulders so that I could see the action clearly. Then as I got older, it was a case of me sitting on the wall perimeter around the pitch, making it easier for me to run on and touch my beloved players. West Ham were by then pushing up into what was then the First Division and I couldn't get enough football in those days.

At school I was captain of the football team and I enjoyed most sports, including being in the cricket team. I also did a bit of amateur boxing as a youngster but it was always a case of football being the winner. People used to say to me that if I stick with the boxing it was a quicker way of making money but soccer was my first love: no doubt about that. We used to kick a ball about during the dinner hour and in the playground after home time. I think I wanted to be a professional from the time I could walk. I started out as a right back when I was very young but was moved to left-back and later on I was again to change position.

The May family subsequently moved to Dagenham, also in Essex, and that really is where my football career started seriously. Local lads like Terry Venables and Martin Peters were stars of school boy football when I was the same age and that's where I got to know them both as opponents, years before our eventual careers in the game. Lads such as Martin, Geoff Hurst, Bobby Moore and myself all played the game as kids but it wasn't a career that was regarded as very appealing as there was little money in the game. I turned out for a number of amateur teams that played on either a Saturday or Sunday: Cortina FC being a side in the Dagenham and District Sunday League I played for as a striker. They used to play their matches at both Parsoles Park and Central Park in Dagenham.

Another side I did well in was called Heath United. They also played their matches at Central Park but folded by the 1964/ 1965 season. As a forward for them I managed to score 53 goals, and my sister still has the trophies I won with them at her home today.

I joined dad working full-time at the meat market, moving great sides of beef, whole pigs, sheep and more, some weighing up to 300-500 lbs. This is where I developed my physique which would help me when I moved into the professional football world a little later. I loved working at Smithfield and was known as 'Little Joe' and the place was full of genuine characters. Its still there today and has been established for more than eight hundred years, marking it out as the oldest market in London. A lot of pro boxers worked there over the years including the future British lightweight Ron Barton, Henry Cooper's brother Jim and in a slightly different field, one Maurice Micklewhite aka Michael Caine.

My burgeoning prowess on the pitch might have been decent enough but on two wheels I was certainly less confident. During my time at the meat market I acquired a little scooter to get me back and forth in the era when London streets would often be washed down overnight. My size wasn't that convenient whilst riding the thing and when I attempted to stop at a traffic light the bike skidded away from under me. I didn't dare ride it again after that; well, not until a holiday in the 1980s with equally hazardous results.

On that occasion, me and Marlene hired a scooter whilst over in Cyprus. We decided to go and visit the northern tip of the country which at that time was controlled by the Turkish government. To get there, we took the beach road. It suddenly turned into sand and finding myself unable to break in time; with poor Marlene on the back, we ended up in a prickly hedge.

Marlene is the lady that knows me best. She says when people meet me, I've always got a smile on my face because I'm the devil incarnate!

Once, I got my ear pierced by my sister when I was working with my dad at Smithfields. Back then things such as this were way more outrageous than they are nowadays. My father was not at all pleased and barked at me, "If you think that you are coming to work with me, you can forget it."

I was brought up in an area where the Kray twins were the local heroes and many had an element of being wild but decent with an ethos of wanting to make a success of their lives. My mother, Minnie, never held me back at all. We thought the world of each other and in fact, both my parents were proud of me. She was of Jewish descent whose family name was Cohen.

Her brother, my uncle Gus, bred greyhounds and many years later Marlene asked me why I hesitated in taking her to meet my mother. "I daren't," came my sheepish reply, "she swears too much!"

A tall, black-haired lady, a typical example of her character came during the 1953 Coronation of Queen Elizabeth II. An estimated 3m lined the streets and mass street parties were enjoyed across the country that year. We had a local procession which all of the children were set to be involved in: myself included. My mother was always encouraging her children to take an active part in the community and this was no exception. The idea was for me to dress up as the teen-aged Indian actor Sabu, popular at the time for his role in the film version of The Jungle Book. Well, my sister looked smashing in her outfit as a pretty dancing girl but my auntie soon arrived to apply gravy browning to my skin to aid my transition into the handsome, elephant-riding child star. My mother attempted to round off my look with a home-made turban adapted from a head scarf made popular with women back in the 1950s. She tied a big knot in it and twisted it around but to my horror it created the effect more like the girls in the munitions factories during the war. With tears in my eyes, she made me join the procession regardless of my protestations.

An incident which illustrates the difference in mentality between my parents came when my father won some money via the Football Pools. He decided to buy a van and a car with the winnings, with the idea of setting up in business. My mother was furious because she wanted to use the money to make a new life abroad.

Another time, I joined the Army Cadets but found that the uniform, especially the trousers, itched because they were made of a coarse material. Mum suggested that I wear my pajama bottoms underneath which was fine in theory but proved tricky during parade when I sweated profusely. People would see my physical presence and think that I was pretty tough but that wasn't really the case back then. As children, we were made to make our beds in a particular way and I guess mum made me a big softie in other areas.

As a boy, I would choose my friends wisely, befriending one lad because his family had a television which I would be invited to watch. Years later during my coaching days with Leicester City in the-late 1970s, Jock Wallace's son, John, remembers that I would eat them out of house and home because his mother Sylvia was such a great cook. So I guess you could say that I have always been an opportunist and able to spot a way to get what I want!

I began my career with Athenian League team Dagenham during the 1960/1961 season wherein I played as a centre-forward, if you can believe that. This was an amateur league containing clubs in and around London. Just before this switch I had been turning out for Southview United FC, then a Sunday team situated in South Essex League. They had spent a couple of years in the Dagenham Sunday League before a switch to the Combination saw us win promotion up into the Premium Division. Our home kit was red and white stripes and one Monday evening fixture found us due to play Wealdstone in the long-established London Senior Cup when our left-back had been injured or suspended and we struggled to find a replacement. As it transpired, this match proved to be the most important of my life. I offered to play the position and honestly I had a blinder! Ted Fenton, a former West Ham United player and manager, happened to be at the game that night and liked what he saw of me. Afterwards, he contacted Dagenham to invite me to come along to the club that he was managing, Division Three's Southend United, for a trial and to train with the squad. I had to get permission for a few days off from my job and thankfully they agreed. That night was strange but like a fairy tale for me. I had played the game out of position and after the game our boss remarked how well I had played and even Ted was asking about me. I was elated: the fact that a respected pro like him was interested in me was pleasing.

Shortly after, I turned out in a couple of reserves matches for them and they put me in to see how well I could cope at the higher level. I had been a regular trainer with Dagenham and knew that my fitness would be monitored at Southend but I was comfortable with that and all that was going on around me: my confidence was blooming. This went well and subsequently another of the games I was to play in was an away, friendly fixture at Oxford United. I was nineteen or so and already married.

The night before the Oxford game my father gave me a hug and told me to do my best as he would have to be up for work at 4 am the next morning. He had always encouraged me to follow my dream of being a professional footballer.

I was happy with the way I played in the match and managed to travel back home to Dagenham with the Southend lads in their team bus. I was buzzing from the game and keen to let my dad know how well I had done. However, before that I noticed that Mr Fenton and his assistant, sitting at the front of the coach as management always did, kept glancing back at me. I assumed that they had been talking about the game and were ready to let me know how satisfied they were with my performance but I was proved to be so wrong.

All of a sudden the manager called me forward and the first question that he asked was if my father had been ill recently. I thought this was strange and I wasn't expecting it at all. It was then that he informed me that my father had died at home earlier that afternoon whilst we had been on our way to the match. I felt numb. I just couldn't believe the fact that he had gone on that day, probably the biggest of my life. He was only fifty three. By the time I did eventually get home most of my family were there and when I saw my mother I just hugged her.

I remembered during the match that the loudspeaker at the stadium asked Ted to go to the head office as there was a police message waiting for his attention. Half-time duly arrived and he decided to keep me on the pitch and relay the terrible news after the ninety minutes. That was a decision that I thanked him for and will always remember.

I turned out in the Football Combination for the club and recall a meeting with Birmingham where I faced a right winger called Mike Halliwell. This 'flying machine' was equally matched by myself and I continued in another couple of games as a full back.

Soon after, Mr Fenton telephoned me at home and said that he was pleased with what he had seen of me so far and that he would like me to be a professional with Southend United: fantastic. This was something both me and my father had always wanted and aspired to for me but I had lost something as well. I know he would have been very proud.

FOOTBALL LEAGUE DIVISION 4

Southend United v. Port Vale

No. 7   **FRIDAY, 14th OCTOBER, 1966**   K.O. 7.30 p.m.

Official Programme 6d.

Above: Southend programme. I'm first left, middle row.
We won the match against a Vale side managed by Stanley Matthews.

2
LIFE AS A PROFESSIONAL FOOTBALLER

After giving notice to quit my job at Smithfield, with my boss and many co-workers having wished me well, I was now doing something I loved and actually getting paid: a professional footballer. People often say that it must be great making it as a 'pro'; all the financial rewards and so on but I didn't look at it that way. My attitude was I had become one when I would still have gladly continued playing the game for nothing. Money back in the mid-1960s wasn't the be all and end all and, of course, nothing like it is today. I signed a twelve months contract and coming from the amateur game could not expect to be earning a massive salary as I hadn't proven myself yet. It was not easy for me in the beginning, what with previously training two nights a week whilst holding down a full-time job to suddenly switching to a five-day schedule as a full-timer. But I was fit and loved every minute of it.

Southend United is a club in Essex whilst Dagenham was probably then the biggest amateur club in the area. A number of West Ham players lived locally, as did Ted Fenton and the club would scout for players in and around east London and Essex.

I had my heroes; Bobby Moore was head of the list and was someone I used to think could walk on water. I admired the man very much and players like subsequent World Cup hat-trick hero Geoff Hurst also impressed me. Along with Martin Peters & Hurst, all three had come through the famous Academy of Football at West Ham originally started by Mr Fenton when he managed the Upton Park-based club. Regarded nowadays as being far ahead of his time in terms of training and dietary methods, Ted made certain that players had options for their post-playing days. This was done by getting them to take their coaching badges and was something I did myself after my playing career was winding down. Bobby was truly my favourite player of all time. He had made his way up the youth ranks at West Ham United and during his fifteen-year playing career captained England to our one and only World Cup success at Wembley in 1966. Most people forget that they also reached the quarter-finals in the 1970 tournament too. Bob collected 108 caps for his country and during the twilight period of his playing days he had a spell in the U.S soccer league a little after I had been out there in 1976 with Chicago Sting (more of that in a later chapter). Pele regarded him as the greatest defender he ever came up against: some accolade. Coincidentally, Bobby was later in charge of the Blues of Southend during his brief and unsuccessful tenure as manager there. But as a player, his legendary status remains with the 'Bobby Moore stand' at the West Ham ground dedicated to his legacy. As part of Alf Ramsey's '66 World Cup winners, a terrace chant at the Hammers ground used to go, "I remember Wembley, when West Ham beat West Germany. Peters one & Geoffrey three, and Bobby got his O.B.E!" There is also a bronze statue featuring him, Peters, Hurst and fellow defender Ray Wilson in the local area commemorating their iconic win: a fine tribute.

I began in the reserves at Southend for a few months and by this point I had switched to being a full-back instead of a striker. However, I have to say that it didn't matter to me as I would have played anywhere so long as I was selected for the team. Frankie Banks also played with me in the reserves and overall, he went on to make more than 90 first-team appearances as a 'Shrimper.' And only recently has he retired from being involved with the club. But returning we were selected to play in a third round F.A Cup match against Rotherham United in January 1966. The crowd that day was a healthy 10,644 and our skipper Terry Bradbury, later a team mate with me at Wrexham, put in an own-goal as we went down to a 3-2 defeat. Banks had been signed by Fenton as a seventeen-year-old and a bit like Harry Griffiths at Swansea, he subsequently performed lots of roles at the club during his many years there and I remember his father was a keen Blues fan too (Southend used to be known as the Blues and the Shrimpers, too). I got a decent write up in the local press for my performance in that cup game and received an early example of colourful journalistic prose describing me as a "giant" with our back line often, "helped out by strong man Eddie May in the Southend defence".

Just as many clubs do now, Southend went abroad for pre-season fixtures but I never made the squad that travelled first time around. When the senior side returned from one of these tours, it became known around Roots Hall that Peter Watson, our established centre-half, had broken his jaw and would be out of action for a couple of months. Pete was the lesser-known brother of future England and Southampton defender Dave. Bill Jones, our reserve team coach, then asked me if I had previously played in this position. I replied that I had not but he told me that the manager wanted to try me there. I agreed and in the next match I was centre half and had a decent game. I was a big guy, tall at 6' 3" and found that the position suited me. I felt comfortable in the role and believed that this was really the beginning for me.

My performance was noted and I made my first team debut away at Colchester United on 20th March 1965. The weather that day was filthy and I came in to replace Lou Costello at left back. We lost the game 3-1 in front of a crowd just short of 3,000. I kept my place and in our next game, a 2-1 victory at our Roots Hall ground attended by a crowd of 2,923. But an early game I particularly remember was a home meeting with Workington, then enjoying a stint as a Football League club. Their centre forward that day was an Irish lad called Kit Napier and it was widely known that he was being watched by a number of clubs (he later made his mark at Newcastle United & Brighton, and for the latter I also remember playing against him too). I can honestly say that I didn't give him a kick of the ball all game. Here I was, aged twenty two, having started as a striker then a full back and now a centre-half: so much was happening to me at the time, the death of my father, switching position, signing pro and thrust into the first XI that I was just glad that the goalkeeper didn't get injured as I would probably have had to play there!

I had to get used to playing in front of a much bigger crowd when I made it into the first team, whilst in the reserves we would get maybe a thousand or so. And when you are a new guy, I found that the United fans were pretty tolerant of me. If I made a mistake, they wouldn't get on my back as they knew that I had just become a professional. If you gave the ball away, they would moan, I didn't have a problem with that: all these things you take on board. I was what might be termed a 'bread and butter' player: I did my job and that was it. I was a tough centre half, not particularly skillful but I felt that I did not have to be in this particular guise. I was able to keep my place in the team because I held this attitude.

I very quickly made a lot of friends in the team and we soon met each others families as they would often attend home matches. I was fortunate to become good pals with Andy Smillie and Mick Beesley, both strikers and former West Ham players, who helped me through the early days of adjusting to life as a full-time pro. Andy was an Essex lad too and would take me in for training as I was still living in Dagenham. Terry Bradbury was at the club from 1962 -1966 and subsequently became a team mate once again when we both moved on to play for Wrexham.

Married life for me and my first wife saw us living with my parents initially until Southend offered us a club house. I was at Smithfields, she was then living in Plaistow, near West Ham's ground and we met at a dancehall in Dagenham where they held a popular event every Wednesday evening that a lot of people used to travel far and wide to attend. It was a bit like the Lyceum in London.

We had been going out together on a few dates and after about six months, decided to get married because she was pregnant. Times were then that you had to get married. She wasn't a football fan but she knew of my serious interest in the game.

I signed a one year contract, the norm for those days, and had a weekly wage of about £25. That was near the same amount that I was on at the meat market but we got by. My mother was a cleaner at a hospital and her pay combined with mine meant that we scraped by in the time before I got married. United did provide a club house after Linda and I had married, a three bedroom bungalow in our case, which was what they did back then. We raised a family of two boys and a daughter, all of whom now live in north Wales. My sons never followed me in to football (although one did play for his school team).

By the start of the 1965/66 season, a managerial change occurred at Southend with Ted Fenton departing in May '65 after four years in charge. As a manager with us, Ted had led the club across close to two hundred games, winning sixty nine of them. In his place came an unusual gentleman called Alvan Williams in the April.

Mr. Williams was a very tough Welshman and had moved into management with Hartlepool before switching to Southend. He was totally different from Ted, who was straight-forward and strict in his manner. I had thought to myself that he was a very good judge of character and someone who would always give you encouragement and put an arm around you, if you needed it. As a manger you have to be a natural. I went on to work with many throughout my career and found that plain speaking really works: it was a case of "If you do this for me, then you are in the team, if you don't then you will not be etc". It wasn't a case of me following anybody as far as managerial technique was concerned: I think it was my will to win. This was to be my belief, my mantra, if you will.

In the 1966/67 season we successfully maintained our status in the league by finishing in sixth spot. I got a goal in a decent 4-0 defeat of Aldershot, in mid-February, and hit the winner against Newport County, also in that same month. Many moons later I would experience a most uncomfortable spell as manager with this Welsh club. Curiously, for the Aldershot game, all our half back line scored a goal-a- piece.

Back to Alvan, he was a man that soon earned the respect from all his players and I will always remember our first bout of pre-season training with him. He gave us an eight mile road run to do and he was in the top five all the way through. On the pitch, we lost twenty eight matches and managed to win nineteen but this failed to keep us up and we were relegated into the Fourth Division. I was to establish myself as a centre half from this season and managed to play in thirty three games. For our opening fixture we faced Swansea Town (later to change their name to the now more familiar 'City') and we beat them 2-0 at home. Unfortunately, a terrible 1-9 dubbing away at Brighton & Hove Albion soon followed (that result remains a club record as the heaviest defeat experienced by any Southend United team to this day). Both the Swans and Peterborough also put five past us during that campaign too. It was during this season that I broke my nose in an away game with Bradford but managed to stay on for the rest of the game. A noteworthy visitor to our place was a Port Vale side managed by the great Stanley Matthews. At that stage in the campaign, we were second in the table whilst Wrexham and Newport County were fourth and ninth, respectively. We beat Vale handsomely. 4-1.

At the close of that campaign, Alvan left the club to take up the managerial mantle at Wrexham F.C. I was sad to see him go as I got on very well with him because I think we recognized similarities in how we both played as footballers. He was a big, tough fella and a 100% winner. For him, winning was the only thing. He was hugely competitive and ambitious, with a first-class attitude that I very much related to. He had also been a former footballer himself with Bury and enjoyed a season as a Wrexham player across their 1956/57 league campaign. As Southend boss, Alvan selected teams for eighty six fixtures and won thirty six of them. He also managed a club in Llandudno at some time where he was player-manager and a former team mate of his there remembers his team-talk. "They might be faster than us lads," he remembers in a correspondence with the author. "But remember, they can't run without legs."

I don't know if that was true or not but my working association with the man was not yet over, as out of the blue he offered Southend £5,000 for me, a fee that was later accepted. I was called in by our then-manager Ernie Shepherd, also another former footballer, and informed of this development. I remember thinking that five grand was a lot of money at the time.

Soon after this, I met up with Alvan at Wrexham to discuss personal terms. I was still happy at Southend but content at the thought of again playing for him.

This all occurred during pre-season and after having a look around their Racecourse ground, I signed for them there and then.

Stepping back into that final season with United, I got one of the seven goals in a rousing 7-1 home win against Workington, in March. It was a performance seen by a big crowd at Roots Hall, nearly 14,000; across a season that saw us win twenty one games.

I went on to turn out for the Shrimpers across one hundred and seventeen league and cup games and netted three times during my time there. One old fan from those days recently described me thus, "An excellent player, tall and gangling but very secure at centre half...'

In all the time I played for them, unlike my uncle, my mother never once saw me perform. She said that she would worry too much about possibly seeing me get injured. I daren't imagine what she would have made of me if I had progressed with my boxing career!

Above photos: *After signing from Southend in 1968, I became an established player in the heart of the Wrexham defence and on to becoming captain. I'm in the top row of both pictures.*

Photographs courtesy of Wrexham Leader.

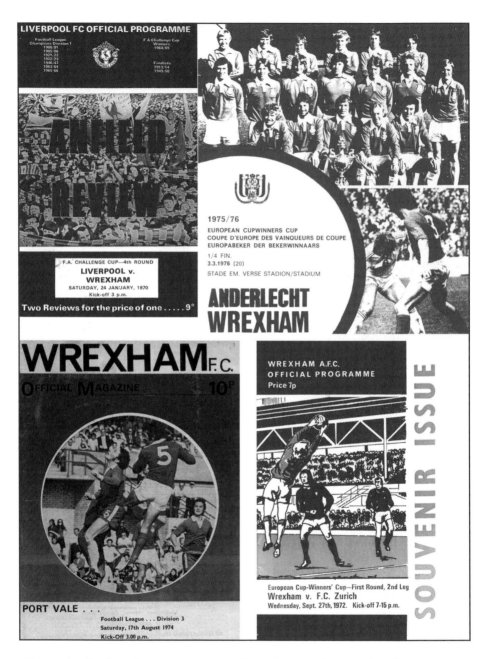

Above: A collection of programme covers featuring Wrexham against the likes of Liverpool, Anderlecht, FC Zurich and domestic opponents, Port Vale.

Above: Success came for Wrexham via the European Cup Winners' Cup
and a meeting with Belgian champions Anderlecht.

Despite success on the field with Wrexham, we were still struggling with attendances at the Racecourse and so this car sticker campaign was launched with me in Lord Kitchener pose. It was given away with the home programme for our first game of the season against Port Vale, which I missed through injury.

Courtesy of Wrexham FC.

3
IT'S MAY DAY
WREXHAM AND AMERICAN EDDIE

'Eddie, Eddie, Eddie...kill, kill, kill...Eddie kill, Eddie kill...Eddie, Eddie, Eddie...kill, kill, kill.' *(Wrexham supporters' chant)*

I signed an initial one year contract for Fourth Division side Wrexham in 1968 via a healthy £5,000 transfer fee paid to Southend United for my services. I thought that was a fair sum for the time. John Neal, a team mate at Roots Hall previously, had left United when Alvan Williams moved to Wrexham. John had been coming to the end of his playing career when he signed for Southend in November 1962 and would garner great success with Wrexham at the Racecourse across the nine seasons he was in charge across 1968 -1977. He made a decent name as a manager before moving on to take charge at Middlesbrough and later, Chelsea. As a player, he made a hundred appearances for Southend between 1959 and 1962 after almost the same amount for Aston Villa.

The pre-season training regime at Wrexham included an annual stint at Aberystwyth. Situated on the west coast of Wales, it is primarily known as a University town and the home of the National Library. We stayed at the university and the squad trained or should I say, strained, on the sand dunes whilst various friendly fixtures were also arranged to get the squad back in to shape following the summer break. The town is sandwiched between two beaches and three hills and I have to say that running on the sand there was tough but it certainly helped build up your stamina. Training and being away together meant that we all quickly gelled and team spirit was strong: everybody played for each other. John was the coach and you could talk to him easily.

My switch to Wrexham felt right as in Alvan Williams I was turning out for a man who liked the way I played and with whom I got on well. This hadn't been the case for every player, as at Southend, fellow defender Frankie Banks remembers Alvan, a son of a preacher, in a rather different light. "In my opinion he was a bully and I had no respect for the man." However, the atmosphere in the dressing room was good and with Terry Bradbury as captain that first season, I didn't regret the move and in fact, enjoyed every minute there across the prevailing eight years. Terry established himself as a firm favorite with the fans at Wrexham as an old wing half. He had formerly been captain at Southend where he was a player for four years, when I was coming through the ranks.

The Racecourse was a compact little ground and was very basic back then. It was yet to see the stands that they now have at the club back in the mid-1960s when I was playing there. I know that more redevelopment occurred in the mid-1970s but I had left the club by then so only ever saw it as a visitor. A record attendance was a 35,000 gate for an international fixture and international players were known to have enjoyed playing at the ground. The club wanted to facilitate such fixtures for the Welsh national side on a regular basis so improvements were later made. In all my years there, the dressing rooms never seemed to be refurbished though.

My debut came in the form of a 2-1 away defeat at Aldershot on a greasy pitch, prior to a mid-week meeting with Port Vale at home. We beat them 2-0 and went on an undefeated run of five games thereafter.

For the first six months, I stayed in a hotel until being offered a club house which was when my family came to join me for what was to be a fantastic professional time at the Racecourse. I rejoined Mr Williams at the club eventually alongside a trio of former Shrimpers from Southend United FC which most notably included the aforementioned Bradbury, who arrived in 1967, and John Neal and Ray Smith. The latter was a decent goal scorer at all his clubs and had been top of the goal scoring chart at Southend in the 1966/67 season. I soon got to be good mates with many of my team mates and one in particular, Arfon Griffiths, known by the team as 'The General' we remain so to this very day. He remembers my arrival at the Robins very well, "Eddie was one of four players brought to Wrexham from Southend by our then-manager, Alvan Williams, who himself had moved on from that club previously. He was a commanding centre half for us and became the rock in our defense. When he arrived his game was a little rough around the edges but Eddie turned into a very good player for Wrexham. He was, and still is, a larger than life character in both size and personality, possessing an enthusiasm for the game which was subsequently communicated via his team talks when he became captain."

Arfon, dubbed the 'Prince of Wales' by the fans, has achieved a great deal in the game but is a very modest man. As a player, he was a wide man with two good feet, maybe not the biggest of lads but he had a big heart and wanted to win: always. He had the right attitude for a professional footballer. A midfield dynamo, he made his debut for Wrexham as a seventeen-year-old in 1959 and went on to make nearly six hundred appearances.

In between, he went to off to Arsenal for an eighteen -month period before returning to the Racecourse and remaining as a player through to 1979. He scored 120 goals for the club and in 2006 was made its Honorary Club President.

Back in the mid-1960s, our families would occasionally socialize along with a number of others as the club was known as a family one back then. Arfon still lives in Wrexham today and we talk on the phone every now and then, often discussing the present state of the club/ team. If they arrange a function to which former players are invited, we usually get to see each other at these events too.

Although my mother could not face the possibility of seeing me injured playing, my family would sometimes come and watch me play in the recognizable red of a Wrexham shirt. The Robins or Reds, as they are known, had been bottom of the League in 1966 but by the time I arrived, for the 1968/69 campaign, the team finished in ninth position (out of a possible twenty four). This was a slight decline on the two previous seasons. My future club, Swansea; then known as Swansea Town, followed closely behind. There was not a great deal of difference in points total between us and champions Doncaster Rovers: they finished on fifty nine whilst we accumulated fifty points from the forty six league fixtures. To demonstrate how close the division was, we had beaten Rovers 3-1 at our place and drawn away. I got four goals across this first season.

The fans chant about me used in the opening of this chapter was a common one voiced during this next season. Max Chard, an avid Wrexham supporter was then a school boy in the mid-1960s and remembers me as being, "An iconic figure, great captain, man mountain and rock at centre-half. Eddie was a true, hard but fair leader. An unforgettable character on the pitch and the foundation from whom the very useful football team was built around." Max can picture me going up into the opposition's box whenever we had a corner and the chant would begin! Let him tell you more. "Eddie would then rise and head many a ball, some finding the net. Thinking back, he was a pioneer of the attacking centre half and in this day I do not remember many if any, defenders ever crossing the half way line." It is funny how people can remember different things from the same event, isn't it?

1969/70 SEASON

"COME ON WITHOUT, COME ON WITHIN,

YOU'VE NOT SEEN NOTHING LIKE THE MIGHTY EDWIN!"

That was a fans' chant that they created from the Manfred Mann hit The Mighty Quinn, a popular record at the time. What a memorable campaign this one was for Wrexham: we never lost at all in either the league or cup games at home all season long. The pre-season regime for this campaign again culminated at Aberystwyth for another bout of desert abuse followed by training at home prior to the start of the new adventure. Alvan Williams had been sacked after sixty one games in charge with twenty six wins. He later became a pub landlord and was awarded a lifetime achievement award in 2003 by the North Wales Football Association for his contribution to local football.

Now led by the thirty-eight-year-old John Neal, we suffered only four away defeats in our first twenty one games. This was to be a great advancement for the club as we won promotion as runners-up and we also did well in both the League Cup and F.A. Cup. At home, we were formidable: winning more than nineteen times in both the League and cup fixtures and hitting a record eighty four goals, the highest in any division. Sides such as Southend, Bradford and York City were all seen off with our biggest result being a 6-2 hammering of Darlington at the end of March '70. Also in that same month, an incident occurred that is forever etched in the mind of Wrexham fan Max Chard. It was an away fixture with Crewe Alexander on a particularly wet Wednesday night when we beat them 3-2. Max was there and he describes seeing the game. "At 2-2, Eddie had been stamped and studded down his back whilst down on his knees on the muddy pitch. It was a particularly cowardly attack, off the ball, which went unpunished by the referee. This seemed to happen a lot back then. However, soon after the Crewe lad was left in a heap in the muck as Eddie scored the late winner, via a corner. On his way back to the halfway line, Eddie passed the said player who was still lying there and looked at him and gave him the two fingered salute. A job well done and clearly seen by all those that had to." Cardiff's infamous striker Robin Friday would perform a similar act at Ninian Park in a match with Luton Town in the mid-1970s (being on that subsequent occasion aimed towards the Luton 'keeper, Aleksic).

More success was to come thanks to the League Cup where we saw to Crewe Alexandra (a 1-0 win against a club also in our same division) and Charlton Athletic (2-0) in earlier rounds. Charlton were then a Division Two side whilst we were two lower so anticipation for who we might meet in the third round was immense. I remember our Club Secretary came running like a mad man to the training ground and called the boss over to tell him that we had been drawn to play the mighty Manchester United at Old Trafford. We were elated and couldn't wait for the tie, a Tuesday evening kick-off on 23rd September 1969.

United had won the European Cup in 1968 and had concluded their season as runners-up in the First Division (the equivalent of the Premiership today).

Writing in the nine pence match day programme, their manager Sir Matt Busby labeled us 'worthy opponents.' His team had just drawn with Leeds and beaten Liverpool in their league campaign whilst our own form was pretty good: five wins in our last five games in a division that contained sides like Grimsby Town and Brentford. The Wrexham team photo featured in the United programme showed me in the back row, a good head taller than my immediate team mates and their description of me as 'a big, strong defender' proved apt.

Often opponents and sometimes team-mates, would call me all kinds of names and they weren't the only ones! The press was also keen to give me a label such as 'Iron Man'. David Lovett, a football reporter at the time termed me "the big boy from Epping." At 6' 3", my height was obviously a help with regards to headers but the most important thing to be good in the air is your timing, heading the ball at your highest point and this comes with practice.

Before stepping out of the tunnel at Old Trafford, I thought its 'do or die' for us here. Kicking off, we went 1-0 up thanks to Ray Smith. Brian Kidd then equalized for United. I remember going up for a corner, which as you will know by now I often did, with about fifteen minutes left, and I scored. Unfortunately it was disallowed for a pushing infringement and then George Best got the winner for them from the resulting free-kick. I have never seen a player with the ability to change direction so swiftly as 'Bestie' did. It was amazing to see. His legs were like rubber and he was easily the best player I have ever played against. I would wholeheartedly agree with England's World Cup winning 'keeper Gordon Banks who aptly termed him a 'football genius'.

As captain, it was my task to attend the toss-up just before kick-off to decide which end either side would play from and I did this at Man United. Bobby Charlton and I shook hands and he gave me a look that said to me, "What's a small team like you doing playing against one like this?" I still thought it a joy to shake hands with such a distinguished player. Sir Matt, who knew little about us before the cup meeting, was suitably impressed afterwards. Incidentally, our team included a trio of former United players in the starting XI. The gate for that evening was an astounding 48,315.

I know that I definitely caught the attention of United, as by the early-1970s there was a strong rumour in the press that they were looking to sign me. My name had been linked with a number of clubs at the time including Everton but the United interest never came to anything concrete. In fact, they were to sign Jim Holton, a lad from Shrewsbury Town instead.

Holton was a full Scottish international and just like myself, later had a spell in the blossoming American Soccer League in the 1970s. Another march forward occurred in the FA Cup too, when we beat Hartlepool by a 3-1 score line and Spennymore United, at their ground, 4-1. All this came prior to a meeting with Norwich City, at Carrow Road, on the third day of January, 1970. We were developing an early reputation as a real giant-killing side and this continued as I scored our first goal and my mate Arfon nabbed the other in a surprise 2-1 triumph. I enjoyed this game and was to play exceedingly well, so much so that as I have said, I got a goal and had a part in our other one too. Match reports of the time revelled in our victory against a Second Division club [we were two leagues lower] as no one thought there was going to be an upset that afternoon. I seemed to get all the plaudits and was voted man of the match. "It's May day as Wrexham earn great win at Norwich" rang one report, whilst others included, "Skipper May is cup hero: and "It's May the magnificent"

Not only had we met Manchester United in a previous cup game this season but for the fourth round of the League Cup we were drawn to meet Liverpool away, at Anfield, for a feisty Saturday afternoon encounter scheduled for 24 January. Everybody was saying to me that if you win the toss, you must defend the Kop for the first half as they were known for preferring to attack it in the second. I did indeed win the toss and we kicked-off attacking that end as planned. Their captain was the sturdy Ron Yates, and when we met on the pitch, he said "Hey big man". I replied, "Hi Ron."

Back when the novelty of cup matches drew huge crowds; our away meeting with Liverpool saw 54,096 crammed into their ground that day. The home fans were silenced when we went 1-0 up thanks to a strong header by the ever-dependable Ray Smith. He rose above the defence to score in front of the legendary Kop, overflowing with the die hard Liverpool fanatics or Kopites as they are known, swaying back and forth in the days when standing was a near religion. Our First Division opponents proved too strong for us in the second half and went on to win 3-1 with one of their goals coming from future football pundit Ian St John. We had held out until the fiftieth minute when their equalizer arrived. Many were suitably impressed with our performance, including the local press there which commented, "It will be a long, long time before Anfield forgets little Wrexham." I have to say that it was a joy playing against the likes of Roger Hunt that afternoon and despite the result it was another grand experience for me and the lads.

In all my time as a Wrexham player, I scored more than thirty times, mainly via headers. But probably the most valuable one occurred in a mid-April League fixture at the Racecourse against Oldham Athletic. My header, in the ninety-second minute, sent in by a cross from Albert Kinsey, saw the game finish at 1-1 and clinch promotion back up into the Third Division. The crowd went wild and in their joy, spontaneously invaded the pitch, which they did upon many an occasion. The delight on my face was captured by a pitch-side press photographer and remains a smashing memento to an enthralling season campaign. There is also another famous photo with Arfon looking on as the supporters literally covered me. We were promoted as runners-up in spite of having three games remaining to be played and had amazingly been unbeaten at home throughout the whole season up until this fixture: impressive with the likes of Notts County, Newport, Port Vale and Scunthorpe in the division alongside us. A super crowd totaling nearly 12,000 was there and heard me make a tongue-in-cheek apology afterwards for leaving it so late to score. Collectively, we hit eighty four goals that season and were runners-up in the league, a single point behind Chesterfield. A tremendous gate of 19,602 had watched a 1-1 draw with Port Vale on 25th October. Vale eventually closed their season's campaign in fourth position whilst Swansea were on the up and finished in third spot just behind us. Wrexham completed the 'double' winning at home and away, over five sides this campaign: Bradford, Hartlepool, Newport County, Northampton and Scunthorpe United. Reds fan M.A. Morris created a poem titled In Praise of Wrexham which appeared in a special souvenir insert in the Wrexham Leader newspaper. Here's what he wrote about me:

"IN THE CENTRE OUR CAPTAIN, BIG EDDIE MAY,

LIKE THE ROCK OF GIBRALTAR, KEEPS OPPONENTS AT BAY,

AND WHEN HE GOES UP FOR A CORNER OR A THROW,

HE MAKES GOALS AND SCORES THEM AS MANY TEAMS KNOW..."

1970/ 71 SEASON

Moving into a new decade, the club was now in Division Three with former assistant John Neal stepping up into the managerial hot seat after the departure of Alvan Williams. It was the first of his nine seasons in charge after having become first team coach back in 1967.

John was a bit different from Alvan; being a much quieter man by nature in his first job in management. Let my team-mate Arfon reflect on their contrasting personalities, "The two were very different people: chalk and cheese.

Alvan was an abrupt personality and ruled the club by fear whilst John was a quiet man with a better knowledge as a coach and a more considered understanding of the game. When Alvan came to Wrexham there were many things wrong at the club and he succeeded in sorting out a lot of them before John became the manager. The latter benefited from the former and was able to enhance the progress of the club thereafter." Arfon also recalls things at the Racecourse being good at first when he himself had arrived there back in 1959 followed by a few years of struggle.

Our first friendly this season was one that I will never forget: it was against Southern League side Hereford United at their place on a very wet night. That 'Gentle Giant' and Welsh football great, John Charles was by then their player-manager after signing for them in July 1966 via a transfer from Cardiff City. Big John made his name at Leeds United before enhancing his superstar status via spells with Italian clubs Juventus and Roma. He also had the distinction of being the youngest player to be capped by Wales when he had made his debut in a red shirt as an eighteen-year-old. Swansea-born John was a man I had seen play and admired tremendously, as did most people in the game. With Terry Bradbury having left Wrexham, before we went out on the pitch all the players were wondering who was going to be the new captain. As we assembled and all stood up, John Neal told me to take the lads out and that was the start of my captaincy. Returning to the other John, at thirty nine, Charles may have been coming to the end of his playing career (he eventually hung up his huge boots in 1974) but I couldn't get anywhere near him that night! John would jump for the ball and you would wonder how he could get such height. John kept calling me a 'big bugger' but he was quite a physical presence himself also at 6' 3" like myself. He showed such agility on the ball and even though I had played against him previously, I will always remember him from this game. It was a shame that not many were there that night to see the match.

There is a popular misconception, thanks to the internet predominantly, that all my goals for Wrexham came via headers, and I would like to state that this is just not true. I did actually score in other ways but going up for free kicks and corners was a recognized part of my game throughout my playing career. My best ever strike in a red shirt was in a 2-2 draw with Fulham at the Racecourse early in the new year of 1971. We had beaten Port Vale on Boxing Day and just a few days later, after enjoying a string of decent results against sides such as Bury, Plymouth Argyle and Tranmere Rovers, Wrexham would motion on to finish the season in a respectable 9th place; this after stepping up a division. For the

Saturday afternoon match with Fulham, runners-up in the league, fans could pick up a programme for the game for a shilling and I got a cracking goal against their number one, Tony Macedo. As a 'keeper, Tony was by then a big favourite with his club and had been at Craven Cottage since the late-1950s. Our visitors that afternoon were regarded as one of the best sides in Division Three at the time (when Aston Villa were also in the same league). The visitors went 0-2 up by half-time before a crowd of 9,400 witnessed my moment just after the hour mark. It arrived when I was on the half way line and we had a throw-in from which my team mate tossed the ball towards me. I let it bounce before controlling it with my chest and then volleyed it, watching as my shot went like a rocket right under the bar: real Roy of the Rovers stuff. This 40 yard strike was talked about by fans for years after and I can still remember perfectly after all these years. I was proud to read an un-named reporter for the local Western Mail newspaper record the moment well, "Wrexham's first goal must rank as one of the finest in the history of the Racecourse..."

The trusty Wrexham legend that is Arfon reflects upon my more well-known attribute, "Eddie's reputation for coming up for free kicks and corners was cemented whilst at Wrexham. He would demand the ball be put on his head after running from the centre of the defence up into the opponents' eighteen-yard-box. If you didn't give it to him he would let you know what he thought of you! Eddie's natural size was utilized; he was a strong lad, muscular and could knock people about. Team mates such as Gareth Davies were seen as being better footballers but each player had his part to play in the make-up of the side. Neal was keen to push the development of youngsters into the first team with the likes of Joey Jones and Mickey Thomas coming through. The team dynamic consisted of four or five experienced players such as Eddie and myself, alongside the youngsters."

"MAY DAY SHOCK FOR VILLA."

That was the headline from the Wrexham Leader newspaper for a surprise victory in our penultimate game of the season. We travelled to the Midlands to meet the mighty Villa and recorded a decent 3-4 away win at their impressive Villa Park ground. The Midlands-based club had been relegated from the Second Division the previous year but were no easy pushovers. For us, this cracking result came after a run of 8 games without defeat including wins against Mansfield Town and Reading. I performed well in the match and was involved in three of our four goals. Villa ended their campaign in fourth place whilst Wrexham settled in nicely for a ninth spot and would remain in the division until the subsequent 1977/78 promotion winning season that took them up into the old Second Division.

In the domestic Welsh Cup we made it all the way through to the two-leg final and came up against Cardiff City who defeated us 4-1 on aggregate. Mel Sutton was playing in the City side for the final and he was to subsequently move and join up with us at the Racecourse with great success. Reaching the final was some progression for us, having been eliminated in the sixth round stage across the two previous seasons.

1971/ 72 SEASON

As the new decade progressed Wrexham built upon their status as the dominant Welsh club but only as recently as 1966 we had been bottom of the Football League, a position that Swansea City also had to endure. Welsh Cup winning success came for us in May '72 with an overall 3-2 aggregate defeat of rivals Cardiff City. The Bluebirds had beaten us in the final of the previous season as I stated but we had much better luck this time round. In the semi-final, we defeated Newport County 2-0 at home in a game in which I had a real blinder.

I netted our first goal in a result that would see us meet Cardiff, who defeated Rhyl, in the final. A local newspaper report noted my "air born menace" in that game with County. For the first leg of the final, played at the Racecourse, we won 2-1 whilst the return ended all-square at 1-1. Match attendances for the former was 6,984 and 6,508 for the latter. Coming in to the competition at the Fifth Round, we beat Oswestry Town 2-0 then Aberystwyth Town handsomely via a 6-2 score line and then Newport on the way to lifting the beautiful trophy.

The present Wrexham side continued a long heritage of cup success in the competition which dated back to the club lifting the inaugural cup in 1877 (a 1-0 defeat of 'Druids' at Wrexham but not at our Racecourse ground). Next to the FA Cup, the Welsh Cup is the oldest domestic football competition in the world and Wrexham have won the trophy more than any other Welsh club. Coincidentally, I won the cup twice as a player with Wrexham and also as a coach with Cardiff some years later.

On the domestic front, it was not the most memorable of campaigns, the season closed with us sixteenth in the division but we did complete the 'double' over Swansea City in the league. Aston Villa won the league on seventy points this season whilst we were back on forty points collected via sixteen wins and thirteen draws.

1972/73 SEASON

The Welsh Cup saw amateur sides compete with the-then four professional clubs (which then included Newport County whom in recent years lost their Football League status) and upsets would occasionally occur. People used to say that winning the trophy was an easy way to get in to the European Cup Winners' Cup; this may have been so but you are still your nation's cup winners, so we valued it. Usually it was always us or Cardiff that won it most years. We had beaten them in the Welsh Cup final in May '71 and it was to be our first venture into Europe, a competition in which British teams had a decent record. Rangers were the present holders and Chelsea, Man City, West Ham and Spurs had all won the trophy.

Our League fixtures commenced in the usual August with a visit from my old club Southend, whom we beat 1-0 on the opening Saturday. After winning the Welsh Cup at the close of the last season, Wrexham were rewarded with automatic qualification into the European Cup Winners' Cup. Our inaugural game against continental opposition in the Cup Winners' Cup would be against five-times domestic Swiss side F.C. Zurich. They had arrived in the tournament as runners-up in their 1971/72 season and we were given no hope of bringing back anything from the initial away game. The competition worked on a two leg basis, home and away, and utilized the aggregate score method. So if you managed to nick an away goal or two, this often proved vital for progressing to the next round.

It was my first time abroad when we travelled to Switzerland, being some years before taking the Leicester City youth team to France, Holland and Belgium. This season would be a new experience playing against better players and in bigger grounds. Wrexham were a Third Division club that found its self playing against teams whose domestic status was much higher than theirs. The opponents were either champions or cup winners and really did play a higher class of football than us.

In the first round, first leg, we were drawn away and so travelled to their Letzigrund stadium in September '72. Wrexham were then fifth in Division Three whilst Zurich were second in the Swiss Division One, with a half-dozen internationals in their team. Our homegrown young stars Joey Jones and Mickey Thomas came along with the first team and both have since stated how terrified they were to be involved. Joey was on the bench whilst the eighteen-year-old midfield dynamo Mickey was selected for the first XI: neither had been away from the UK before.

The European Cup Winners' Cup had been introduced in 1961 and Zurich would go on to meet our future cup opposition, Anderlecht, in the same tournament, the following season. The former had won their domestic league and cup a number of times in the 1970s and would go on to reach the semi-final stage in the 1976/77 season. But returning to the Zurich match, a gate of 6,500 saw us come away with a 1-1 draw, with Albert Kinsey nabbing an all-important equalizer for us. Unfortunately, our official supporter's party didn't arrive until after the game had started and I have to say that the role of the Wrexham fans was a major part in our success, they cheered us on and even John Neal acknowledged their significance. I had a decent match and two weeks later on 27 September, we met them at the Racecourse for the second leg. A terrific crowd of 18,189 crammed in to witness our 2-1 win thanks to goals by Billy Ashcroft and Mel Sutton. This proved the cue for another friendly pitch invasion. I remember that I got cautioned during the match.

For our next opponents, we were awarded a tough draw with veteran European campaigners Hajduk Split. Children could get in for 20p to see us but I didn't play as I was out with an ankle problem. Nonetheless, that end of October encounter saw Wrexham put in a 3-1 success deflated only by the subsequent 2-0 defeat at their place in Yugoslavia. A massive 25,000 were at their Stadion Plinara ground to see us go out on the away goals rule (aggregate away goals coming in to play and being of additional value). We competed rigorously with them, culminating with a full melee on the pitch after my shirt had been tugged by one of their lot. Split had six internationals in their side but had just been beaten 9-2 in the league when we played them! After seeing off Zurich in an early round, we won the tie against Split at the Racecourse 3-1 but got knocked-out on the aggregate score, where away goals counted for extra, via a 2-0 defeat at their place. During the away fixture, I had found myself clean through on goal when I was blatantly fouled by two of their defenders. A dubious Polish referee did not award Wrexham a penalty in an unpleasant match which was very intimidating for us. In the local Leader newspaper back at home, a sports reporter that experienced the hostility too and termed the game as the "Scandal in Split."

Some domestic success was achieved with Wrexham retaining the Welsh Cup by beating Cardiff 2-1, also on aggregate.

During the season I enjoyed a brief switch to the number nine shirt instead of my customary number five, due to an injury to our usual striker big Billy Ashcroft. Billy later moved on to Middlesborough where he was signed by one

John Neal after he too had been tempted away from the Racecourse. But I was happy up front and would also do the same in a spell in the American Soccer in the subsequent summer of 1975.

Back at Wrexham, I scored via a non-header in our 1-1 draw with Rotherham and managed another in a January '73 draw with Bristol Rovers. Other strikes included one against Aston Villa, the most memorable being in our 3-4 away win at Villa Park back in May 1971. That one was a header and in a game I played very well in and was also involved in three of our goals. My reputation as a late goal threat was growing, with one reporter oddly noting my prowess for "aerial ballet tactics."

1973/74 SEASON

"ONE OF THE MOST MEMORABLE."

Manager John Neal, who won two Bell's Manger of the Month awards across a season within which Arfon nabbed eleven goals for us. In the League, then our fourth season in the Third Division, we went on a smashing run of form at home by winning five out of the first seven fixtures (including a League Cup tie with Port Vale), with an 18:6 goals ratio. Regrettably, our away form was the opposite: five defeats, a win and two draws.

In the FA Cup, we again performed well and progressed thanks to wins against an out of form Shrewsbury Town (after a replay), Rotherham United (a 3-0 success), Crystal Palace (2-0 at their place) and a victory over Middlesborough. For this tie, we were pitted against a 'Boro' side then managed by World Cup winner Jack Charlton, we were somehow coerced into an unusual publicity team shot, being 'dressed for the kill as the undertakers'. Whatever, it worked and we beat them at home in January '74 by a 1-0 score line. A terrific 20, 612 had made the game a sell-out recorded in record time and were there that wet afternoon to see the win against a side that had been enjoying a good run of form in Division Two. It was a terrible day to play football, with the wind and rain creating a muddy playing surface. I cleared the ball off our goal line and Arfon laid on our winning goal for Brian Tinnion to net. Future Liverpool legend Graeme Souness was in their side that afternoon and their manager acknowledged the defeat, reporting that Wrexham was "A good, well-balanced team."

Next came Southampton and for this fifth round tie, played out on another muddy pitch, seen by a gate of 24,000 we came away with an excellent 0-1 away result. It was the Saints' biggest gate of the season and saw Wrexham resplendent in our lucky white kit (we always seemed to perform well when wearing this). Southampton were then a Division One club and included the brilliant England player Mick Channon and veteran star Terry Paine in their side.

Then came Burnley in the second week of March '74. Astonishingly we were two games away from a Wembley cup final date! It was reported in the press that the players were each offered Ford Capri cars as an enticement to win the match and we walked out from the changing rooms wearing new tracksuits with each of the player's names on the back ala Leeds United. A deflected goal cost us the game in this 1-0 away defeat. The Clarets were then a Division One club and had an up-and-coming Welsh youngster called Leighton James in their team. The lads were all gutted to go out of the competition thanks to a freakish goal that was accredited to Frank Casper but which actually went in off our player Davie Fogg. That single strike at Turf Moor thus concluded our involvement in the competition. In our cup run that season we beat sides managed by the likes of Messers Charlton, Lawrie McMenemy and former West Ham man Malcolm Allison. We ended the season in our domestic league in fourth position narrowly missing promotion. Oldham won the league followed closely by Bristol Rovers and York City, both on sixty one points, with Wrexham frustratingly only a single point behind them after gathering fifty six points.

1974/ 75 SEASON

'WREXHAM - YOUR CLUB NEEDS YOU!'

The powers-that-be at the Racecourse utilized my face in a spoof of the famous Lord Kitchener recruitment poster pose as Wrexham sought to drum up support for the club. It was used as a car sticker given away with the match day programme for the opening game of the season, a tricky meeting with Port Vale which ended 2-2. Despite our exploits in Europe across the previous season where we had reached the quarter finals stage of the European Cup Winners' Cup, home attendances were down; hence the above campaign to get bodies through the turnstiles.

At the start of this season, I had amassed two hundred and sixty two appearances for Wrexham and managed to net twenty seven goals. By May '75 we closed the season in an unlucky for some, thirteenth position out of twenty four. We did pop in some goals especially against Plymouth Argyle and Watford at home (both being 5-1 wins). Domestic success was achieved by Wrexham via the Welsh Cup by defeating Cardiff 5-2 on aggregate following a 2-3 defeat of

City at Ninian Park in which I didn't feature due to injury problems.

1975/ 76 SEASON

So much had gone on across the prevailing seasons for me at Wrexham and for the 1975/76 season, my final campaign in a red shirt, I enjoyed my football hugely. In my penultimate campaign I had missed many games due to a niggling ankle injury but for this final stretch I was an ever-present in the line-up, be it in the League or various cup tournaments; I played in the lot. This was really due to the three months that I spent in America playing for the North American Soccer League (N.A.S.L) side Chicago Sting during the summer break in the English domestic leagues. The family came too and we were housed in the Churchill hotel that was situated about five minutes from Lake Michigan in the Gold Coast region.

This all came about thanks to a UK-based group that was recruiting players for the U.S League and a representative had been suitably impressed with my performances for Wrexham, so much so that I was offered a contract. I got permission from the club and was off for a great adventure in the States. Chicago had returned to the domestic league in 1975 and took their name from the 1973 film, The Sting. I was now in my early-thirties but I swear that I was two yards quicker than the players at home when I subsequently returned to play for Wrexham.

Bill Foulkes was the 'Sting' manager when I joined them in the Central Division in 1975. As a Manchester United player from 1950-71 he also continued as a coach there too. Bill came from a family of sportsmen and was a survivor of the tragic Munich air crash which took the lives of a number of his team mates. Known collectively as the 'Busby Babes' Bill remained heavily affected by the events for many years.

He was in the United side that whacked Wrexham 0-5 at the Racecourse in January 1957. That was an F.A Cup fourth round fixture seen by 34,445 with Bill playing alongside the great Duncan Edwards. It was one of his 679 appearances for United which places him at number 3 in the all-time appearances table for the Reds (only Bobbie Charlton and Ryan Giggs have played more games than Bill). Subsequently, Sting was the first of his three U.S teams that he managed prior to his move to Norway where he worked for a further eight years. He also had jobs in Scandinavia and Japan and now lives in retirement in Sale. Coincidentally, after my playing days had come to a close, I had a stint as a coach over there in the former, too.

He was a tough task master: in keeping with his time as a United centre half and proved to be one tough cookie but if you did your job properly, you were fine. He knew the players that were messing about and those that were carrying the team. The sponsors wanted to see the home-grown American players featuring in the side but Bill didn't like that. He brought decent players over and wanted to play safe with the established British lads.

The 'Sting' had a big staff. The original team captain was a former Bradford City midfielder called Rod Johnson. But he picked up an injury early into the season and Mr Foulkes said to me that I would be taking over the captain's role in the interim. However, even after Rod returned I retained the captaincy.

Predominantly playing on astro turf, occasionally you would run out on grass, specifically at the Tampa Bay Rowdies stadium. The money was alright but primarily, my reason for going over there was to focus on improving my fitness. The astro turf here in the UK is like rock but over there they play American Football on it and there is a spring to the surface. I didn't have any problems with it; the ball bounced true and if you shot, it would run flat and so on.

We weren't scoring enough goals at one point and as usual, I had been coming up for corners as this was one of my strengths as you know. One day in training Bill asked me if I would like to play up front. I told him that I had done so at Wrexham, upon occasion, and so I played as a striker for the Sting after a half-dozen matches had been completed. In one game, which I think was down in Houston, I got two goals and was acknowledged with a man-of-the-match award which I still have somewhere. In all, I notched up a total of a lucky seven goals in eighteen games for them.

The broad mix of players made the league a real cosmopolitan melting pot of virtually every nationality. Our side included players from England, Ireland and Israel in amongst a squad of twenty four. Names such as Eddie Cliff, John Webb and Clive Griffiths all helped shore up the Sting defence whilst I was involved. Webb was a Liverpool-born lad who played a few years of his football over in the States and in all, turned out for Chicago on fifty four occasions. Griffiths was a Pontypridd-born defender whose previous clubs had included Manchester United and Tranmere Rovers (John had played there too previously). He was with the club across a four year period and played more than a hundred times for them.

As for me, I took the number three shirt and the time spent abroad did my fitness a world of good. I returned feeling refreshed and ready to deal with the less colourful upcoming fixtures in a Wrexham shirt at sides like Gillingham, Mansfield and Aldershot.

Before the major league started in America, they had a small league and it wasn't a big thing over there. The bigwigs hit on a plan to improve things and the game took off quite well with the public. I travelled to lots of places across the States including Miami, Baltimore and Florida which was fantastic as we flew everywhere, as such is the vast distances between cities.

It proved a valuable experience for me as in the 1974/75 season I had picked up an ankle injury which had meant that I missed about ten games or so for Wrexham. I had lost a lot of fitness and saw the summer in the States as a way of improving this: which it did very successfully. By the time of the 1975/76 season, my final campaign as a Wrexham player, I was raring to go. I think that I subsequently played in every game for them.

Before going to America I had read that they were looking to bring in international players from established football-playing countries such as the UK. My Wrexham team mate Arfon had gone there and played for Seattle Sounders and did especially well. His success gave me the idea to try my luck too and as mentioned, Wrexham kindly agreed for me to go over for 3 months. Arfon was there in 1975 in a team that also included former Spurs star Mike England. Coincidentally, both would later manage the Welsh national side at different times. As Sounders team mates, they played together against the legendary Pele who had come out of retirement to sign for New York Cosmos in '75 and gave the whole thing much kudos. Arfon proved a great success and turned out for Seattle on fifteen occasions and was included in a 'Best XI' league select. He and I were one of many Brits over there, South African-born Eddie Firmani had been a team mate of mine at Southend in 1965 and was with the Tampa Bay Rowdies as their coach, too.

Ultimately, the trouble with the soccer league over in the States was that teams were going wrong in my understanding by signing players that had been released by their clubs and probably getting older. Names I remember playing alongside at Chicago included Ian Storey Moore, a past Man United and Nottingham Forest name, who was recently working as a chief scout with Aston Villa) and former Millwall man Gordon Hill and a couple of Irish lads too. Gordon had come up via the Athenian League, just like me, and had played some youth games at Southend. He was a lad confident in his natural ability and possessor of a great left foot, and he went on to play for Manchester United and returned to the States for another spell in the 1980s. Gordon liked the country so much that he now resides there. When I was at Sting, he was our top scorer that season on 21. We were in a division that consisted of five teams: St.Louis Stars, Chicago Sting, Denver Dynamos, Dallas Tornado and San Antonio Thunder.

The League being divided in to four divisions: Northern, Central, Eastern and Pacific with twenty teams in all. At the time I played in the States Pele was the one truly great footballer who had been tempted to sign on. Of course, he played for the super glamorous Cosmos and was followed in subsequent seasons by Bobby Moore (San Antonio & Seattle), Johan Cruyff (Los Angeles and Washington), Franz Beckenbauer (Cosmos), Eusebio (Boston Minutemen) and Gordon Banks (Fort Lauderdale) amongst many other journeymen.

But back to my time there, clubs were signing Mexican names, Chilean names and so on. Again, the principal should have been that you still have to do a decent job. A lot of people who played there loved the lifestyle of sunbathing on the beach during the day, training at night when the temperature was cooler and enjoying the many lovely distractions. Although, you still had to put in the time out on the pitch. I think they laid out too much money for named players but eventually I savoured my time there. Attendances were not that great in 1975, despite tickets being as low as $5.00 and averaged 7,000 until peaking at a little over 14,000 by 1979. The Chicago home games were played at the massive Soldier Field complex. Unfortunately 'Sting' just failed to make the play-offs due to a penalty shoot-out defeat by Washington Diplomats and we were runners-up in the division to St.Louis Stars. As a team, we scored thirty nine goals in twenty two games, winning 12 (there were never any drawn games as the Americans always need to have a clear winner or loser).

I think that the American public didn't really 'get' the sport and a number of changes were implemented to make the games more exciting for them. Elements such as a shoot-out for matches that concluded in a draw; alterations to the off-side ruling and a complex points system were all tried. There was a keenness to assess sports stars and in the soccer league they monitored pretty much every aspect of the game. Looking at my score card, I managed to score a lucky seven times, penciling-in three assists and gained seventeen points during the course of my season there. However, I had needed to play regularly due to having not done so thanks to the ankle injury sustained back at Wrexham. Over in America, the medics would not strap my weak ankle up in one complete bandage but used strips of bandage to allow better movement. It definitely helped me.

I would have liked to have gone back and played again there but with the interest shown in me by Swansea City in 1976, I never did.

After winning the Welsh Cup at the close of the previous season, Wrexham were back in the European Cup Winners' Cup with another September fixture kicking off the campaign. The Swedish Third Division side IF Djurgardens visited the Racecourse and were beaten 2-1. Just over 9,000 were there that night. At our place we were getting okay attendances but for the second leg tie, a paltry 1,769 saw me get booked but we did progress to the next round.

The little known Polish side Stal Rzeszow were struggling with their domestic league form when we met them on 22 September '75 at the Racecourse. I hit the post with a header and we were much better than them and finished the game with a 2-0 result. For the Bonfire night second leg, the squad flew to Poland from Manchester airport, to visit an area known for its steel-making, for what turned out to be a much harder return fixture. It was a long, arduous trip across 1,200 miles to meet this First Division side but it was worth it. A group of die hard supporters also traveled to the match with us on the same plane. We were then playing in the Third Division and the game attracted a terrific crowd of 22,000. Fortunately for us, we secured a passage to the next round via a 3-1 aggregate, having shared the spoils 1-1 on the night.

The aggregate victory over Rzeszow meant that we made history as it was the first time that a Third Division club had progressed to the quarter-finals of a major European tournament. Excitingly, Wrexham next got drawn against Belgian champions RSC Anderlecht for a quarter final encounter on 3 March '76 at the Parc Astrid stadium. The team flew to Belgium from Liverpool airport and were photographed wearing a giant red and white scarf that fitted us all collectively! It was recorded that some 1,200 welsh fans made the trip over to Brussels to attend the match. Incidentally, the eventual final itself was scheduled to be played there at the National stadium.

We competed in that away tie in front of a 35,000 crowd on that Wednesday night. Their star player, Van Binst, hit the winner to set up a lively return leg on the 17th of that same month. Anderlecht were then enjoying their best years and you have to remember that they had nine Dutch and Belgian internationals including one Robbie Rensenbrink in their side. He and his strike partner, Gilbert Van Binst, had hit thirty goals between them already that season. Also, some of the Dutch boys had played well in the 1974 World Cup finals and soon after, Rensenbrink would go on to be awarded the prestigious Golden Boot football award in 1976.

Despite such stacked odds, I did quite well in the air battles with my European counterparts. Anderlecht won the match 1-0 and I got booked for retaliation after Van Binst fouled me. The national press back home favourably reported our endeavours as a Division Three side, "Sheer guts and Wrexham hold their heads high" was how the Liverpool Daily Post reported in their 4 March 1976 match review. The Anderlecht fans demonstrated their distain at their side's performance by booing their side off the pitch at full time. Even those inside the club were not too optimistic, with their coach Hans Croon commenting after the result, "This was a massive result for Wrexham tonight and we have no more than a 50-50 chance now." He also singled out the threat that Billy Ashcroft posed to his team and viewed Arfon as our "most elegant player." So here we were, competing against Anderlecht with the return match seeing our highest attendance at the Racecourse that season with nearly 20,000 eagerly anticipating the next 90 minutes. Previously, our local derbies with Chester had proved most popular with fans.

Such is the wonder of football, we went 1-0 up just after an hour and overall put in a respectable team performance on what was a tense night for the players. With thirteen minutes left that man Rensenbrink, who had done very little across the whole game, struck their winner but I know that our supporters appreciated our efforts. What I learnt from these two games was that when they were losing, the Belgian side didn't panic. They played their football. I'll never forget Rensenbrink especially. At Wrexham, Mickey Adams, now manager of Principality Building Society Welsh premier League side Caerswys, was often put on dangerous players and he did a brilliant job all game. They got a free kick and it flew in after taking a deflection which shot past Mickey and was met by Rensenbrink who hit it with a twenty yard shot to make it 1-1. Into the seventieth minute we were doing okay but their skilful striker Van Binst got the ball and motioning to shoot, brought the ball down whilst the defenders turned their backs. But instead of shooting, he shaped to shoot: then smashed the winner. We went out 2-1. It was a great experience to play in a competition against these players and we couldn't quite believe that we were competing with professionals of this class. However, to go out was unfortunate as we felt that we had performed very well.

The thrill of these European meetings was not only revelled in by us players but also by the supporters. One of them, Martin Jones, commented on the BBC north east Wales website, "My dad took me at the age of twelve, up until then I was a Man United fan but from that moment I have followed Wrexham. I was on dad's shoulders due to the large crowd and the fact that we were at the back of the Kop stand, but the atmosphere was electric and the noise deafening. A night I will always remember." Anderlecht went on to win the trophy by beating my childhood favourites West Ham by 4-2.

We had a good run in the tournament with a lot of tough games often against famous sides. And I think that we were taken aback when we won the first two rounds. The fact that we went and played at Anderlecht's magnificent stadium and saw the crowd and having absorbed the overall build up to the game, we realized that this was a bit different from what we were used to. Saying that, Wrexham never went anywhere and let themselves down. We were classed as an industrious team who made it tough for sides to beat. We never got whacked. I think that the players felt proud to be playing against such teams too. Here's what my fellow team mate Arfon thinks of those games. "These were a wonderful experience for us all and we never once disgraced ourselves even against the big clubs of the time. We had a good side and developed a reputation for playing attractive football that was good to watch and being an overall decent football side. It wasn't a question of riding our luck as we were not outclassed in any European tie."

Wrexham seemed to be the darlings of the sports media this campaign culminating in the lads visiting the Granada studios where they film Coronation Street. I remember that me and Arfon Griffiths had our photo taken in the Rovers Return pub, standing next to the legendary Bet Lynch (the curvaceous Julie Goodyear) and Hilda Ogden (Jean Alexander). Leaning against the bar, I nearly did a Del Boy from that classic scene in Only Fools and Horses; as the set was not as solid as it looked and I nearly fell over it as the bar was not actually stuck down!

My physical prowess was often utilized on the pitch for Wrexham but on occasion, would also be used off it. When the club had a storming run in the F.A Cup, me and Arfon were photographed with a director's wife in a terribly clichéd pose. I remember it now: I wore a shirt which was open to my navel, positioned next to this beautiful lady and a grand piano. Poor Arfon stood there with his hands in his pockets next to us! If you see the photograph today, you would understand how for some years after I was known as "Medallion Man" by Marlene's children! It was all down to Charles Roberts, a flamboyant director at the Racecourse and responsible for the various publicity opportunities to promote Wrexham F.C. (such as the two mentioned above). These were usually when the team was enjoying a fruitful cup run and the media seemed to lap them up. Charles subsequently moved on to become chairman at Bangor City when Arfon became manager at Wrexham.

Arfon was the type of person that appreciated people acting in a professional manner, be it on the pitch or in training. He was a bit like me in that way: maybe that's why we got on so well. Neither of us liked players not training properly. Arfon had principals and you had to act professionally. People looked upon the two of us as the mainstay of the team. If you look at any publicity photographs about Wrexham we are always in them. I think that we were the oldest at the time and we brought the best out of our team mates. Neither he nor I shied away from keeping the younger element of the team in hand, as well as passing on our footballing knowledge and understanding of the game. Some youngsters naturally believed that after having broken into the First XI that they knew everything there was to know about certain things but we spoke to them soon enough. The season saw a return visit to my old Roots Hall stomping ground, where Southend played, in February marked by a 1-1 result in a game played on a Sunday due to the power crisis and three-day week situation of the period.

Cardiff City often used to win the Welsh Cup before Wrexham started to achieve success in the competition when I was a player with them. I don't think there was a lot of difference between the two clubs. Sometimes City played in a higher division, whilst we made a good name for ourselves, both home and away. There has always been a rivalry between the original four professional Welsh clubs (back when Newport County could still be included). And as I said, often we were in different divisions but the Welsh Cup brought us together. When I played in the red shirt of Wrexham, the 'big four' competed in the cup but nowadays this is no longer possible. From a league point of view, another local derby was with Chester, which was only about 12 miles away from us.

We had a good blend of young players and seasoned pros at the Racecourse. Our manager, John Neal, did a great job in gelling us together. The combination worked and we had a well-balanced team. I had first known John at Southend, where we were team mates. Wrexham had a decent youth team and he signed people like Mel Sutton, who had been released by Cardiff. Mel had played a number of times in the European Cup Winners' Cup for them so brought a great deal of experience upon joining us. He did a great job and was a good professional.

Players like Joey Jones and Mickey Thomas were apprentices at Wrexham and soon gained international recognition for Wales. They were outstanding youngsters and when they came into the first team, they contributed a lot. Joey was a tough full back who didn't take any prisoners whilst little Mickey, at 5 ft 5", was a bundle of energy and a very skillful player. He had made his way up the ranks at the club prior to turning pro in 1972 and was steadily on the up only for his own demons to cause him problems. Both lads went on to great club success at Liverpool and Manchester United respectively. They integrated well with others like myself and Arfon. Joey has described Thomas, a lifelong pal, as being "Physically strong and tough. A man's, man." That's a label subsequently given to myself. Both later returned to the club in the guise of player and coach respectively.

Concluding a traumatic campaign we failed to gain promotion up to Division Two and closed the campaign in sixth position. Local rivals Cardiff City gained promotion, behind eventual champions Hereford United who we had beaten 2-1 at home this season. We hadn't managed to beat City but did manage a 1-1 draw at our place. Familiar faces in the side such as Billy Ashcroft, a fans favourite, left at the season close as did manager John Neal and myself. Arfon Griffiths took over as manager after I moved on to. Arfon is a legend at Wrexham, a great player and was previously John's assistant at the Racecourse. Both of us are included in the Hall of Fame display at Wrexham's Racecourse ground.

I had gone to Cardiff to take my F.A. coaching badges where I had to attend a residential course at Sophia Gardens, near the city centre. Little did I know that John Neal and Harry Griffiths, the then-Swansea boss, had already been discussing my future. I had seen 'H', as he was known, at a couple of games previously and he tried to tempt me to join the Swans as a player-coach. I had seen a Wales international at Swansea's Vetch Field ground shortly before, I think it was against Northern Ireland and Harry followed me in to the gents and offered the player-coach role. I got the qualification, now a prerequisite for any would-be manager in the modern game, and thought about his offer long and hard as I saw it as a possible next step in my career.

Returning to the Racecourse, as the season came to a close I was 33 and the Robins had just signed John Roberts, a past Arsenal and Wales international at centre half. Consequently, speaking with the boss, I was told that the club had intended to offer me a renewed contract but that it was my decision as to what I wanted to do. The player-coach development seemed a natural step up for me and John agreed. It was then that I decided to accept the offer from Swansea after Harry Griffiths had contacted Wrexham to table a formal offer. My final League appearance for the club, at home, was a 2-2 with Southend United, funnily enough.

As I will do with my period in charge of Cardiff City in a later chapter, I thought I would give you a flavour of the pick of the sportsmen that I enjoyed playing alongside whilst at Wrexham.

1 David Gaskell

Dave dominated his penalty area and would go through opponents when he came for the ball. He came to the club in 1969 after some years at Manchester United and kept goal at the Racecourse for four years before a move to South Africa. Back in his day, keepers would ordinarily wear heavy gloves but Dave was different, he had a lovely, thin pair of white ones given to him on match day by an on-duty policeman! He said that he could get a better feel for the ball with them. Quite a character.

2 Steve Ingle

A Bradford-born defender who left my first club, Southend, in 1967 to join us at Wrexham. Steve was built like a boxer and was very quick for a big man. A strong running footballer, he was better going forward than defending but his qualities far out weighed his lesser skills. During the winding down of his playing career Steve played in South Africa for the same team as Dave Gaskell, the Arcadia Shepherds.

3 Gareth Davies

A very quiet player who didn't talk a lot during a game but did his job well. He was handy in the team as he used to pick up things that I missed. I think he played more than six hundred times for the club.

4 Eddie May

A cracking player in the heart of the defense! Writing in his autobiography (Oh Joey, Joey! My Life in Football, Blake, 2005) former team mate Joey reflected upon life at the Racecourse. "Eddie May and Arfon (Griffiths) were the pick (of the players). They were the established stars and, at the back, Eddie in particular was one of the best I ever played with. Nobody messed with Big Eddie and he'd die for Wrexham. He was hard, the God father of the Third Division... " Another reds team mate, Gareth Davies, was also complimentary. "(Eddie was) a fabulous player - strong in the air a good competitor, and very quick for his size."

5 Joey Jones

A whole-hearted player that fans at the Racecourse loved. Joey hated losing games and was a good man to have as a defender. His debut came in January 1973 in a Welsh Cup defeat to Chester. He established himself in the team by the 1973/74 season and later made the transition to a higher division to play for Liverpool. That says it all about him as a player.

6 Arfon Griffiths

There's not much more that can possibly be said about 'The General' as we called him in the dressing room at Wrexham FC. As a player and manager, Arfon served the club well across many years and today holds the honorary title of club President. He was awarded an n M.B.E in 1976 for his services to Welsh football.

7 Mel Sutton

At Wrexham we used to come up against Mel when he was turning out for our local rivals Cardiff City. He was a tough-tackling player always looking to create things on the pitch. We subsequently signed him from the Bluebirds. There wasn't much too him but he never pulled out of a tackle. Always one of Cardiff's better players at the time.

8 Micky Evans

A dedicated footballer who succeeded in any position but started off at Wrexham as a forward when joining us in 1966. A bit like me and Arfon, in as much as he would keep the players in line and would have his say in the dressing room. A deep-thinking player, he now lives and works in Caersws, north Wales, where in recent times he was manager of the local club there. His career ended due to a back injury. A good lad.

9 Mickey Thomas

'Noddy' was like Joey Jones; football was a breath of fresh air to him. He would weave his way through a couple of players and do a couple of tricks and then return and try to beat the guy again: he was that kind of player. Mickey was well-liked at Wrexham and enjoyed geeing the crowd up. We called him 'Noddy' because when he ran with the ball, he would always nod his head. Arfon sold him to Manchester United because Wrexham needed the money. I know Mickey had a spell in American football and when John Neal took him to Chelsea he still had to do pre-season training on the beach at Aberystwyth but Mickey was always super-fit. Like me, he boxed as a youngster too. He would make a tricky quiz question, "Which Wrexham player started and finished his career with the club and had 12 more clubs in between time?": the answer is Mickey!

10 Billy Ashcroft

A Liverpool-born lad who hit more than seventy goals for Wrexham across his eight seasons with the club. He was a big guy by the time he was 20/ 21 after coming up through as an apprentice in 1970. Billy was good in the air but he could have been more physical in his game due to his size. He was the type of personality that you could get the ball up to and he was big enough to hold it. I think that he could have been a more dedicated footballer; he didn't realize how lucky he was to be a professional footballer. If he had a fault it was that he didn't think enough about the game. Bill had a happy-go-lucky attitude and was popular in the dressing room due to his perfect impression of Tommy Cooper. Someone said that the two were related but I don't know if that was true. He had a lot of skill for a man of his stature. Later signed for Middlesborough for a transfer fee of £120,000 when John Neal was in charge there. In more recent times Billy ran a pub in Southport.

11 Graham Whittle

An all-action footballer: great going forward, possessor of a savage shot and could get up in the air, even though he wasn't that big. Two good feet; Graham could charge forward but if an attack broke down, he could get back and help out in defence. Professional in his attitude to the game, he was a hard-worker in training and had made his way up through the ranks of youth football in Merseyside. Knee problems saw him quit the game before he was thirty after making his Wrexham debut in 1971. His brother, Alan, was also a pro, at Everton.

12 Dave Stallman

A silky kind of footballer. Very much left-footed who played up front with Billy Ashcroft. A full Welsh international, he was spotted by John Neal accidentally when the latter was scouting for another player. Dave preferred to have the ball played to his feet. Had a lot of skill and went out of the game far too early due to terrible bad luck with various injuries. Hit quite a few goals for Wrexham when we stormed through to the quarter-finals stage of the F.A Cup in 1974. Dave then moved to Everton for decent money and has been termed by many as one of the games 'might-have-beans'.

13 Brian Tinnion

A striker to begin with when he joined us from his home-town club Workington in 1968 via a then-club record fee of £140,000. He had blistering pace but was too small for a striker and so John Neal put him on the right-side of the middle four. People like Mel Sutton and Arfon used to change the play to Brian and once he controlled the ball and ran at players, nine times out of ten, he succeeded in getting in a cross. Brian left in 1976 and across his period as a Wrexham player he played close to three hundred times. He later played in the States for the New York Cosmos, no less.

14 David Fogg

'Foggier' could play anywhere in the back four and was similar to Joey Jones in that respect. A Liverpool lad like Billy Ashcroft and Dave Stallman, he was a good guy to have in your team as he worked hard. He was converted from a striker into a defender and made his debut for us in 1971. In later years he remained in the game in a coaching capacity at a number of clubs including Everton and Shrewsbury Town.

If you are wondering why there seems to be a proliferation of Liverpudlian names in my list, the reason why this is so is because Wrexham had scouts in that area and every school holiday we would have promising youngsters come across from there and join us. Geographically, Liverpool is less than an hour's drive from our north Wales base. Back to matters at the club, a team mate at the Racecourse during my entire career there, Arfon Griffiths stepped up to become manager at Wrexham in 1977, a year after I left. It was whilst at Charlton in the early-1980s that an offer came in for me which resulted in becoming the worst decision that I ever made in my football career. Arfon left the post in 1981 to take up the managerial role with Wales and I was working at Charlton alongside Lennie Lawrence. One day, he called me into his office and said, "Right, things are happening for you." I replied, "Oh yeah?" and Len continued, "Wrexham have been on the phone and want to interview you for the job as manager." I gulped in anticipation. "What you've done for them is standing you in a good position to get it." So the next day I made my way up to north Wales from London for an interview. But I made a big bloomer: I tried to be greedy. I overpriced myself with the board at the Racecourse because I felt that my success there as a player coupled with my recent employment with Charlton, at that time situated in a higher division, was how I based my worth.

I have regretted this ever since. It was the wrong approach and I lost the job because it was subsequently given to Dixie McNeill. He had been transferred to Wrexham in 1977, a year after I had signed for Swansea City. Dixie played one hundred and sixty seven games for the club prior to filling the managerial role in 1985.

Top: *I spent the summer of 1975 with Chicago Sting in the American Soccer League. I'm in the middle row, behind the number 8 player below.*

Above: *Swansea City team photo for the 1976/1977 season in Division Four. I would spent the final two seasons of my playing career with the Swans and was there when John Toshack arrived.*

4
LIFE ON THE UP AS A 'SWAN'

Only a few years before I signed for Swansea City, the club had successfully sought re-election to the Football League after finishing at the bottom of Division Four at the close of the 1973/74 season. I signed for them in August '76 after being with Wrexham for eight years and had enjoyed a great final season there but I was ready for the next part of my career, in readiness for their 1976/77 Fourth Division campaign. My move down south to Swansea, a one hundred and thirty nine mile trek from north Wales, brought some changes to my life and I thought "Here we go again!" after buying a property from my new chairman Malcolm Struel.

John Charles had been working at their then-present ground, the Vetch Field, for a couple of years in a coaching capacity but left the club just as I moved there so I never got to work with him unfortunately. He had an outstanding reputation amongst his fellow pros and remains well-loved by fans today. Similarly, I think just like my hero Bobby Moore, a good reader of the game, John's success in coaching/ managerial roles never quite succeeded in replicating his own high playing standards.

The facilities at Swansea weren't as good in comparison to what I had known at Wrexham, where some recent modernization had occurred. At the Vetch in 1976 the place hadn't been touched. The playing surface at the Racecourse was also much better but here it was comfortable enough.

Young names such as Mel's son, Jeremy Charles, Alan Curtis and Robbie James and Wyndham Evans all began to establish themselves in the first team when I was there. And you could see that Jeremy was going to be a good player even at the tender age of sixteen when he made his debut with a hat trick against Newport County at the start of this season. 'Charlo' could have played up front or defense but he liked to be in midfield best. The Swans manager Harry Griffiths used him more as a midfielder than anywhere else. He received great encouragement from his father, Mel, himself a legendary name in Welsh football, having served the Swans well for six years as a player. Mel would attend home fixtures and liked to speak his mind after games. He would give you advice. He was a nice guy who gave his young son a lot of positive belief. Griffiths had been quite the goal scorer for Swansea back in the 1950s and played more than four hundred games in a white shirt. And his wife, Gwen, rightly described him as a 'soccer fanatic.' In all, he spent three decades at the Vetch in various guises.

As a Swan, I was an ever-present in the team across the 1976/77 season campaign, establishing myself in a team that included Pat Lally in defense. Pat now works as a regional League Football Education Officer for the Professional Football Association. But back as a team mate, he made 161 appearances for the club before leaving in 1978.

That first season was an interesting one for me and as a team we did well: hitting a record ninety two league goals in Division Four and narrowly missing out on promotion. At the close of the campaign, we beat Cambridge United away but because Bradford had lost at Colchester, it meant that we failed to go up by the narrowest of margins. We performed well as a team and the campaign culminated in the Swans finishing fifth in the table. I think it was a late defeat against Watford that threw us, as we had won nine of our final twelve league games up until an early-May defeat in the last home game (a 1-4 pasting). Attendances at the Vetch Field were averaging out at about 3,000 with visitors including Southend and Newport, in our division.

The blossoming of youngsters coming through at Swansea echoed that at Wrexham where the likes of Joey Jones, Mickey Thomas, Brian Whittle and Bobby Smith had progressed nicely. Both Robbie James and Alan Curtis progressed rapidly at the Vetch and soon developed into fully-fledged Welsh internationals. I later took Robbie to Cardiff some years later whilst I was coach there. He was a great talent, Robbie, and when I heard he had died I was very sad. I was then out of the country. He was a terrific player and team mate. When we again worked together at Ninian Park, I have to say that he did a great job for me. Robbie was very versatile and an industrious footballer whom I liked to play in the middle of the park. When I took him to south Wales, he had previously been filling a role as striker. I played him in midfield or right-side of midfield but more of that later.

Back in June 1977, our chairman Malcolm Struel decreed that Swansea aimed to be in the Second Division within a couple of years. Fans seemed to agree as season tickets sales were booming as we moved into the 1977/78 season. The bookies made us 7-1 favourites to win promotion in a campaign where supporters paid 80p to watch games at the Vetch Field. The previous season had been significant because it was the first time that the club had made a profit in thirteen years. Gate receipts had doubled and things were looking very prosperous but behind-the-scenes there was a big change coming our way.

After completing a season as a player, Harry gave me the new role of player-coach for the oncoming 1977/78 season. It was the fourth season in charge for Harry and from this point forth I became heavily involved in working with the players; from doing the warm-ups, everything. It was all a valuable learning curve whilst I was still playing in the first team too. Doing this kind of work, you really had to be careful that you did not stand about too much and consequently let it affect your own fitness. As a coach, you do have a tendency to be fixed; what with talking to players and other members of the coaching staff around the sidelines, instead of getting in there and doing it yourself. It was a tough job at times.

It was very rare that Harry would come out and look at the team and ask any questions about what I was doing; he just left me to it. He was a jovial guy, very likeable.

Performances were going well on the pitch but off it, Harry was struggling as the boss at Swansea. By October '77 he was sacked by the club and I remember that the fans were furious. It was soon reported that Colin Addison, then manager at Newport, turned down the offer of managing the Swans and so Harry returned to run the team. I was made club captain in November and was assisting with training the first team by then. Also in that month, we met a future club of mine in my post-playing days, Brentford and beat them 2-0 away at their Griffin Park ground. At the end of December, following not a single defeat in November, Mr Griffiths was awarded the manager of the month award and we all ploughed on.

With attendances on the up, Swansea was a club that was definitely going places but by February '78 Harry was finding the job too much and was worried about his future. He had been enjoying working with the youth side and didn't want to have to do the day-to-day stuff of club management feeling it was a young man's job.

Into 1978, we were performing well in the league and national cup competitions: fifteen wins, ten draws and five defeats. Midway into the campaign, rumours abounded that former Cardiff player John Toshack was coming to the club and when he did take over as the new player-manager in March 1978, 'Tosh' dropped Harry down to assistant and I think it really got to him. Officially, of course, the club was saying that what was needed was a new, robust manager to take over but Swansea was his club, it was his home town and when all the changes were made this went some way in breaking his heart.

I had played against John, when he was an established Liverpool player, in Arfon Griffiths' testimonial match at the Racecourse in Wrexham back in July 1971. Bill Shankly brought a strong squad of players down and 'Tosh' had moaned at me for the whole game. I felt that his eventual arrival at the Vetch would mean the end of my career with the club. This was made apparent soon enough when he called me into his office and declared that he would be taking over as the new captain, a role that I had filled. I simply agreed and stated that this was his prerogative.

Arfon was ahead of Toshack in the innovation stakes, as he was already player-coach with Wrexham by the time Toshack began his duties with us on St David's Day 1978. Our first home game with him in charge was a tricky tie with Graham Taylor's Watford on 3 March. There was a great deal of interest in the changes at Swansea and a decent crowd turned out to see the clash. Played out on a terrible Vetch playing surface, we went 2-0 up by half time only for the high-flying visitors to go 2-3 up as the game moved into the second half. That man Alan Curtis struck a late equalizer to finish the game at 3-3. The starting XI for Swansea City that night was as follows: Barber, Evans, Lally, May, Charles, Moore, James, Curtis, Toshack, Bartley.

As the season advanced, good things were happening for us and poor Hartlepool were the recipients of an 8-0 hammering at our place on April Fools Day! Robbie James and 'Curt' both enjoyed hat-tricks but I can't recall who got the match ball.

With only a couple of games to play, on the pitch I enjoyed our performances and promotion out of the Fourth Division looked likely. Tragically, Harry Griffiths died in the treatment room at the Vetch on the day of the penultimate fixture, Scunthorpe United, on 25th April. Harry was forty seven. Speculation was rife that the match might be postponed but the players agreed to play and we won the game 3-1: a great tribute to him. That match was seen by 13,228 whilst our final fixture came in the form of Halifax Town on Saturday 29 April, was to be enjoyed by 16,300 at the Vetch who saw us gain promotion to Division Three via a 2-0 victory. During the match I had a header cleared off the line and another, setting up Alan Curtis, just went wide. Toshack got a goal in the sixty eighth minute and Alan rounded things of nicely in the eighty sixth minute to cement the club's first appearance in the higher division since the 1972/73 season. We were up into the Third Division with fifty six points collected with Watford finishing as champions whilst my old club Southend United was runners-up; followed by ourselves.

There were many matches full of drama and excitement during the course of this advancement and one of special note was a 4-4 against Stockport County in March '77. We were 0-3 down but somehow managed to level the score before the final whistle. Another had to be that resounding 8-0 romp against Hartlepool back on April Fools Day.

When I had taken over the role of player-coach at the outset of the season, I was struggling in games. I felt that I was a yard short from what I was used to. I also felt that I miss-timed things and at about an hour into games I was blowing hard because I hadn't been doing enough training. The funny thing was, when Toshack came to Swansea he brought his own coaching staff and to be fair, this helped me focus purely on my game as they took the coaching sessions. He brought in former Spurs and Swansea player Terry Medwin as his new assistant in May 1978 and I realized then that my days there were numbered. I am not saying anything new when I state that I have never liked the man. I didn't care for the manner in which he had told me of his intentions from the off. However, I was still selected for the first team and it did not bother me that much. I felt that he believed that I had a lot of influence with my team mates and that I might be perceived as a threat to him. This was untrue as I simply continued to get on with my job; same as always. We didn't get on but it didn't worry me much as I had my own plans for the future and when I was ultimately offered a role in Jock Wallace's Leicester City backroom staff. I had to return to the Vetch and inform the club of my new plans as we still had a couple of games left to play in the season. I will talk more about the 'Foxes' soon on but back to the Vetch first.

I knocked on John's office door and didn't give him a chance to mention anything about offering a new contract or not with the Swans. I got in first and told him that I would be leaving at the season close and did not want another contract. The manager asked me what my plans were but I refused to disclose anything as I felt it was none of his business. I got my things together whilst my family remained in Wrexham. Toshack had almost signed for Leicester earlier but had failed a medical.

In all I turned out ninety times in a Swans shirt and played in 44 games across that second and final season. I hit ten goals: the first came in October 1976 during a very cold winter, against a club that I would later manage, Torquay United. Others came against the likes of Newport County, Scunthorpe, Workington, Huddersfield Town, Colchester United, Rochdale, Stockport United and my old team, Wrexham. The last goal I got for the Swans was in an uninspiring 2-1 defeat to Crewe Alexandra seen by a little less than 3,000 in

September 1977. The Newport game was of note as I made my Swansea debut against them in a League Cup victory in August 1976.

However, the match in which I scored against them was, coincidentally, the same score line, a 4-1 Welsh Cup victory in January 1977 spotlighted by an Alan Curtis hat-trick.

It was time for a new direction in my career nearly two hundred miles away with Jock Wallace in Leicester, as their new coach and I was ready.

When the end of a footballer's playing career rears its ugly but inevitable head, it can prove a mighty challenge for many to deal with. You have to suddenly readjust your entire working life and I think that ex-West Ham man Alvin Martin summed it up well, "You are going into unknown territory," commented the former England star and now a pundit on Talk Sport radio. "Some of the guys you thought wouldn't miss it, often did; whilst those that you imagined would, actually didn't."

In the summer months of 1975 when I went to play football in the States with Chicago Sting in the N.A.S.L, Arfon Griffiths and myself were by then the oldest hands at Wrexham and I think our domestic manager at the Racecourse, John Neal, allowed me to go because I was coming to the end of my career. On returning to the UK, as I said before, I really was the fittest that I had ever been. Subsequently, I got offered a coaching role at Leicester, a decent club back then and I realized that this was my next, natural step. Because I went to a big club I thought to myself that I have a chance to stay in football, which was my priority, and you cannot always do so as a player, so you have to move on as a coach. I missed playing but it was a decision I had to make. I could have carried on as a player and then been discarded and left wondering where or what I might do next. Therefore, I was quite pleased about this piece of good fortune in being able to take up a new role as youth team coach with Leicester City.

As a player, superstitions and rituals were rife in preparing for games. I purposely put my shorts on last, seconds before we went out onto the pitch and often, footballers wear the same clothes or lucky tie or put on their left boot before the right. Even at Southend United, when we would run out, I would always try to take in the atmosphere generated by the crowd. By the time I was captain at Wrexham I was always the first one out of the tunnel and would see them all around.

That was especially enjoyable, in particular if the season had been going well for us. "When I was a kid," recollects one supporter in a correspondence with the author, "my dad always took me in the paddock part of the ground (no going into the rough Tech End) and when Eddie ran out from the corner dressing rooms I'd always give him a big cheer and he'd inevitably wave back."

As a defender, I frequently got called a "dirty so-and-so" by the opposition's striker because you are trying to stop them getting through at all costs. You had to make your presence known on the pitch; my size and weight, fourteen stone, meant that people expected me to be physical: I had a reputation for being so. Back in the 1960s and 1970s this was accepted by officials and those in the game but it would not be allowed today. Players get away with things too much in the modern game. I think that there is much more diving than there ever used to be: it gets players into trouble. Some of the sending offs you would never have heard of years ago. Certain players fall down and look as if they've been shot. The game used to be more physical simply because it was allowed to be. You cannot get a whole-hearted tackle in now. If someone is going to lose the ball, nine times out of ten they fall to the floor.

Arfon assisted John Neal at Wrexham for a couple of years before he advanced to management so he had a fair idea of coaching. He had also played at the level he was now involved at and so the transition from playing to coaching/ management was not so difficult. Speaking with him, he will tell you that John helped him to further his insight into the game. Stepping up to a higher level, I never had this parallel but was still fortunate to gain so much at Leicester. As a coach there, sometimes I would take the reserves and I could say whatever I felt about their performances on the pitch but when I sat in with Jock and the first team, he was the one to give the team talk. You could go around and suggest something to individual players but it was all a valid part of my own further education in the game. What makes or breaks you as a coach is how you speak to players and get on to them to implement what you want done on the pitch. As a former player, I could understand this situation. Arfon learnt his trade as a coach at Wrexham but for me the situation was different at Leicester. They were in a higher division than I had played in. I knew what players were about and what abilities they had and if they failed to show this I would voice this with them in an attempt to figure out why this was the case. This would be thrashed out on the training pitch where concerns would be addressed: it was where your mistakes needed to be put right before the next match.

Before I moved to take up my final playing role at Swansea City in 1976, Wrexham had competed in a youth tournament in Lille which I attended. Staying in the same hotel was Jock Wallace, a former goalkeeper who had attained extensive success as Glasgow Rangers manager, winning the European Cup Winners' Cup in 1972 as well as domestic trophies thereafter. We had a good chat about football and I thought no more about it. A soccer-related dinner in

London in 1978 saw both of us being invited guests and again we had another talk. Jock had just taken over at Leicester and he asked me what I doing presently. I told him that I was now at Swansea and that I knew of his move to manage a club in England. "Come and work for me." He suggested. We got on very well and he was a man I admired and so was very proud of being considered by him. He offered to teach me everything he knew, just like Willie Waddell had done with him at Rangers, and when he said that it was an easy decision for me to make: I accepted the offer.

Now that I had retired from playing, I saw this as an exciting new step in my career in the game. I had a full coaching licence and was ready for my coaching education via a legend from Scotland: Mr Jock Wallace. I could not have asked for a better tutor. I was confident in my coaching abilities but what I wanted was to learn about man-management, club organization, youth policies and everything else that could aid me in my quest to be a successful league manager.

Arriving at their Filbert Street ground, I was appointed in the dual role of reserves/youth team coach but during the early months there, I kept thinking that maybe I had retired from playing a little too early. Jock would take away the first team and a few reserves and I would work to structure those that remained. He would make sure that he covered everything; some managers never watched their youth teams or reserves but he inspected both in every game. Mr Wallace believed in youth football and gave great encouragement to the boys in treating them well.

I think I did make the right decision when I moved to Leicester as the grounding and education I received there was phenomenal. It transpired to be a period of learning across the next five years. When I came to join the Foxes, I had been coaching the first team lads at Swansea and felt comfortable in continuing. So the coaching side held no fear but what did was the fact that I was now handling players of a higher standing. As time moved on I began to realize that what I needed more was to learn the ways of club management. I dealt with players like Keith Weller, Alan Birchinall and other well-known names back when only a couple of substitutes were permitted in first team fixtures. Those that found themselves out of the first team squad or had been dropped, could not just sit on the bench like some do nowadays, or up in the stands, they had to play in the reserves. If a player had been out injured, it was common practice for him to have to run out in the reserves before returning for prospective first team selection. Arfon remembers recognizing my love of football back when we were team mates and that I was nuts about the game even then. He wasn't at all surprised to see that I moved into coaching and management subsequently.

At Leicester, when I was there, they had recently come down from the First Division and hence still retained first-class facilities. There was a magnificent training ground, an indoor gymnasium the size of half a football pitch and a floodlit, astro-turf practice pitch (which proved useful for ball work). Jock made sure that these high standards were maintained whilst he was in charge. We also used to have school boy training on some nights in the gym and these lads were impressed with what they saw and heard from the coaching staff. Jock's family were also with him when he took on the managerial post at Leicester and his son, John, was then a teenager, "I think for Dad, on a personal note, it was a great challenge and to be away from the 'Gold-fish bowl' lifestyle in Glasgow when he was in charge of Rangers. Dad could only go to three or four places there, socially, where he and Mum would not be bothered, and of course, at that time the religious divide was very much to the fore, Northern Ireland was for all intents and purposes, at war." John continues. "You have to remember, Leicester at that time in the late 70's/early 80's was a very well-to-do city, with a thriving local industries (rag trade, threads etc). But before moving there, I obviously knew of the team. When Dad arrived he immediately got rid of the older players, and as Eddie has commented, experimented with young players and the more experienced players that remained (there were very few that could handle the training)."

In my youth team I had a player called Gary Lineker and I never met a youngster with so much ambition. He would always listen, give you 100% in training and in matches and soon progressed from youth team to reserves. It wasn't long before he was knocking in the goals for the first team and he was a racing certainty. He was very quick, strong and brave and as he matured, the more powerful he became. By his late-teens you could see that he was developing physically. When we had him aged seventeen he looked quite frail. But all this changed. He would run and had great strength, even getting up in the air to score some headers. Gary wasn't a big lad but his best asset was his pace. He could sprint off the mark and get past defenders. A lot of his goals also came via 1-on-1 scenarios with the 'keeper. Gary was an apprentice at Leicester and was given his debut on New Year's Day 1979 but made his name at City in the early-1980s. His introduction came on a frosty home pitch against Oldham and he played badly out on the right wing rather than the traditional centre forward role that he is remembered for. A boyhood Leicester fan, Gary remembers his time with the club fondly, "There was always a good atmosphere at Filbert Street." He commented on a recent BBC radio documentary, "with a special buzz around the place."

That was a view shared by many. "Paul Ramsey and Paul Friar at that time were super players," says John Wallace before echoing Lineker's comments. "Paul was a good trainer and very serious about his trade. Thinking back it really was a young squad. There was a real buzz amongst the players."

Off the field, Gary did some baby sitting for our two sons and I still enjoy telling people that and would relish in doing so when he was at the height of his career as a Barcelona and England international player. It was whilst he was at the Nou Camp with Barca that Gary was managed by Terry Venables. Nicknamed 'El Tel', we had come across each other back in our school days years before.

John Wallace also remembers "The boy Lineker" as former England star Mick Channon termed him. "Gary occasionally would drop me off after I visited the ground; he had a red Alfa, and drove it as fast as he ran: which was not slow..." Young John trained with us a couple of times and recalls it vividly, "Eddie was first class, he was always constructive with his comments, and had a right go at the players if they dropped their efforts. He always made you want to be involved, I was only having fun, but the apprentices were encouraged, and made to react professionally, he was a great coach."

We would play in the Midlands Cup against the likes of Coventry and Nottingham Forest with first team players in the side who had come down to the reserves if they had been dropped from Jock's starting XI. I would take them to games but I had to let them know that I was not afraid of their status. They needed to know who I was and I made sure that they did. Sometimes players who have been dropped don't perform and on occasion, I had to give them a boot up the backside to let them know that if they wanted to get back into the first team, then they had to prove themselves in my teams. I would make a report for Jock to view and he would take appropriate action.

After a couple of years a guy called Dave Bridgson came in as a youth team coach after having established a reputation in a similar role at Aston Villa. This allowed me to focus on the reserves and because we did it this way, Jock had an extra coach with him. I would look after players in the first team and some of the reserve players, about twenty five or thirty. I also helped Jock with the warm-ups and so forth. This meant that I could see how he worked with first-rate footballers. When Jock first came to Leicester City Football Club, he went through a number of players very quickly and brought a number of youngsters in, enjoying some early success within which I was involved. He was not afraid to give a fledgling lad a chance and didn't doubt his readiness. Jock was always positive and believed in his judgment that after observing a lad play he felt he was ready for a shot in the first team. People would ask if this was a gamble, but it really wasn't: it was belief. And if you believe it and tell the player then you instill in them the idea that he too can do it. I always felt that this was a good thing. Jock held the opinion that you should not be overtly friendly with players, that you needed a professional distance. They had to respect you in your role and from this you would find that they will play for you. It is a policy that I have carried through in subsequent coaching appointments. At Leicester, I found myself working with the same players for a long time, people like the teen-aged Lineker and so on. Jock's pre-season training was really tough but his lads would run through a metaphorical brick wall for him. Just as we had run on the sand at Aberystwyth in my Wrexham days, he introduced similar methods at Leicester: only here he recreated dunes in the guise of a great hill of earth!

Periodically Jock would send me up to Scotland to look for prospective new players and with the success that he had already enjoyed at Rangers, you could understand his way of thinking. He trusted Scottish lads far more than their English counterparts.

Leicester won the Second Division with some ease at the close of the 1979/80 season in a division that included Swansea, Cardiff, Chelsea and Newcastle United. Apart from the keeper and one other, all the players that season were under twenty three years-of-age. Alas they then repeated a familiar pattern of going straight back down after only a season in the top division. But the whole set-up at the club was made for the top league. A season ticket for that year cost fans £33.80 for a seat in the Double Decker stand (coincidentally, Swansea had the same name for their stand at the Vetch Field) and a match day programme was a mere 25p. The club had quite a memorable run in a later season, the 1981/82, by reaching the semi final of the F.A.Cup. That season in Division Two saw Leicester close the campaign in eighth position. Luton Town won the league but relegation came knocking for both Cardiff City and Wrexham.

Jock Wallace was regarded as a father figure to many of the young lads coming through at the club, including one Paul Ramsey. Paul would later work with me at a number of other clubs but let him tell you about life at Leicester. "All the team working on the coaching and management side of things there were 6'3" tall and a formidable bunch. Everyone took their lead from 'Big Jock' and all shared the same principals in football. Jock would instil in me and my team mates the ethos that you have to give everything for the fans, work one hundred percent and demonstrate your commitment. Jock even accepted an invitation to my former youth team in 'Derry. He attended an event there and chatted with the youngsters. I was deeply appreciative in his giving up his time for them. Like Eddie, Jock was a mentor to all of us at Leicester; he was an immense personality and a great talker of the game. Real old school."

Every club has its characters and at Leicester one of ours was a certain Keith Weller. He had been at the club since 1971 and he is a player forever remembered for an item of improvised clothing which he wore for an icy cup match. I think all football fans remember looking in disbelief at the white 'long-johns' tights that he wore under his shorts for the match. Keith wasn't at all bothered about the response so long as he was warm. Nobody else had ever played in such an outfit before and I remember Jock Wallace telling him before the kick off to take them off as he looked like a prized prat! Clearance from the referee had to be obtained and everybody had a good laugh when he ran out on to the pitch. No one could believe it, really. Even seeing clips of the outfit all these years later still evokes the same response from most of us: sheer exasperation.

The great thing about Leicester City under Jock was the flexibility. If he came to watch the youth team play I would be sitting next to the physiotherapist on the bench and he would sit alongside us. He would be quiet as it was my team and it was the same for the reserves. It was a case of letting me get on with things. I felt that he was saying to me in a discreet way, "Go on, learn. Come on, you're learning. What are you going to say, what are you going to do with these players?" He would then come in to the dressing room afterwards and if we had lost the game, I would give them my opinion. He would let me say so before he wanted to speak. When I had stopped, that was it: he would rip into them! But the great thing was when he walked in he didn't take over. He acknowledged that it was your team and let you get on with the job. Jock could be as mellow as anything and as tough as old boots. You could never read him; he liked a man's man.

When we won the Championship, I would like to know what he spent in the transfer market. I know it was a small amount. He signed a couple of Scottish boys, Alan Young & Alan Lee and as I said, by the end of the first season he had begun to put his own stamp on the team. I think that he believed in the value of Scottish players. He felt that you might be a decent enough football player but if you had no aggression in you, then you were no good to him. He felt that a Scotsman would not let him down, that's how it looked. He followed a lineage of Scots managers at Leicester and even today in the Premiership, Sir Alex Ferguson, David Moyes and Alec McLeish continue the pedigree made manifest by the likes of Bill Shankly and Tommy Docherty before them. Scottish bosses worry, they work harder than most too. What I liked about Jock and the others is their aggression. They strive to get the most out of their lads and it is inspiring to work with them.

Back in the 1970s, Showaddywaddy was a popular band and its lead singer Dave Bartram, a locally-born lad, was a big Foxes fan. I was invited to his wedding and he generously presented me with one of his trademark teddy boy-type crepe jackets that he and his band used to wear on stage. For a long time after I enjoyed strutting about in various poses in the mirror whilst wearing it. "He's always been a peacock," says Marlene, someone who was to become a big part of my life in later years at Cardiff City. "I realised that because if I was a vain woman, I wouldn't be able to live in the same house, as I would not be able to get near the mirror! Eddie wouldn't like to have anybody around him that's too vain, as they'd compete."

I have to say that I was shattered when Jock left to return to management up north with Motherwell in 1982. He was a shining light in my life and when he departed I was convinced that I too would soon be away from Filbert Street. "Dad loved it at Leicester," reflects his son, John. "And Mum still wonders what would have happened if they had stayed, instead of going back to Scotland. I recall vividly when he and Dad chatted after scouting missions (sometimes over one of Mum's steak pies at our house); they would dissect the players, pitches, refs, stadium lights! To the very last detail, Eddie had a great memory of names, faces and games. Dad trusted his judgement: full stop."

Gordon Milne came in as new boss and as often happens; he brought in his own coaching staff and ideas. I hadn't known that Jock was about to leave City but afterwards we kept in touch and I think he had some success back there. He had his own assistant up there, which was okay by me. I missed him and his exit had a big effect on my own subsequent departure too.

If you are a good coach, then you can transfer this ability to wherever you are. Jock Wallace taught me so much about managing a club, he would always say, "Remember that, big man." His grasp of tactics and desire for players discipline were first class in my eyes. Players loved him. He was a very proud person and the biggest influence in my professional life. Jock was a very careful man in his ways, and especially when choosing his friends. For me, he is in the same ranks as Bill Shankly. We took to each other immediately.

Jock had an ability to weigh people up very quickly. If he spoke to a player with a vague interest in signing him, after ten minutes talking with him he knew whether or not he wanted him. I was privileged that he invested so much in me at Leicester City.

I have tried to incorporate these ideals too and I think that when you talk to somebody or watch them play or train, if they are dedicated then this is the first thing that you want to see. I don't think that you can observe this so much nowadays as there is such a great deal of money in the game; it's a different world. For a foreign player to come into English football, years ago, was something that just did not happen. Today, people and companies from outside the country are buying English clubs all the time. Again, this is only a recent innovation. Some of them are getting involved but are not lasting too long; you only have to think of recent events at Liverpool and Manchester United to see this. Once upon a time it would have been inconceivable to see a club with such a rich heritage as Liverpool struggling to find new ownership.

I think the situation is snowballing out of control.

But returning back to when Jock left Leicester City, by this time my family was happily settled back in Wrexham and during my tenure at Leicester I would often watch neighbouring Lincoln City matches where I would see Lennie Lawrence, as he would also come and see our matches and so we struck up a friendship. Lennie was then the assistant to Colin Murphy at Sincl Bank and our association would soon develop after I had left Leicester in 1982.

Whilst working in Kenya with African side Gor Mahia, I got a call from Lennie Lawrence back in the UK. It was 1982 and he had just been given the managerial post at Charlton Athletic and said to me that he needed someone with experience to assist him at the club and that's where I came in. Lennie had been assistant to Colin Murphy at Lincoln City and the latter kindly gave me a great reference when Len stepped up at Charlton. Colin is a much-loved name at Lincoln, even to this day, and I appreciated his good words.

Therefore, I jumped at the chance of possibly returning to British football and a deal was subsequently agreed after I had seen out my brief tenure over in East Africa. I was preparing arguably the country's most successful club side for the oncoming national league. They were based in Nairobi and were able to draw on a dedicated fan base from all over the country, with an impressive ground capacity of 30,000. The club got its name not from a region but from a legendary person called Gor K'Ogalo who had the nickname of 'Mahia'. They were then a relatively new organization after only being formed in 1968 but by the time of my involvement with them, they had already won the league on five occasions and the domestic cup twice. I was involved in structuring training matters.

Working at Charlton meant that I was lucky enough to live back at home with my mother in Dagenham. This meant that I could travel across London to get to work at the Valley ground in less than an hour. This also allowed me to nip off and see Southend play as they were managed by my former football hero Bobby Moore.

Like me, Lennie believes vehemently in the fact that you can do all the necessary prep training and tactical work but ultimately your players have to want to play for you out there on the pitch. He has managed across more than a thousand games through his career and is appropriately known in the game as 'Houdini'. This is due to his propensity of keeping clubs up in spite of financial restrictions or on-field problems. I can vouch for this fact thanks to my first hand experience of working with him. Although never a professional footballer, Lennie is a great coach and has a deep knowledge of the game. He was originally the reserve team boss there before being promoted to manager in November 1982 and went on to lead the club for the next nine years. He brought in Alan Simonsen midway through the 1982/83 season which generated a phenomenal amount of press coverage. Known as the 'Great little Dane', he was a full Danish international and former European Footballer of the year winner and people did wonder why such a player would come from Barcelona to a small club like Charlton. Alas we couldn't afford to pay his wages and so Simonsen departed after hitting an impressive 9 goals across 16 appearances. Alan was a top striker and had made a name for himself in Germany and Spain prior to coming to us. It was a glamorous and surprising signing back in the day when foreign players were still considered a colourful novelty.

Whilst I was there, I remember going to a January '84 away fixture at Cardiff City in the Canon Second Division 1983/84 season where we got beat 2-1 (but in the return game at the Valley we won 2-0). We also visited my former club Swansea during that same season at the Vetch in late-February but got beat 1-0. We had faired better at our place, with a 1-1 draw back in the previous October.

It would be via Lennie that future Cardiff favourite Graham Kavanagh was given his debut whilst at the London-based club some years later. 'Kav' turned out for his former boss in an 'Allstars' match at the new Cardiff City stadium in 2009 but more of that later.

At Charlton, Mike Flannagan and Derek Hayles, both legendary names there, were coming to the end of their respective careers by the time I got to the club. 'The Addicks' as they are known, have a tremendous following in an area where there are no other nearby big clubs. We would often be in the Canon Second Division before winning promotion to the old First Division, then sponsored by the Today newspaper.

In the 1980s it was common knowledge that Charlton Athletic had deep financial problems and at times the players did not get paid or were unable to train. New directors came in and many changes were instigated. The club almost folded in 1984 and they did go in to administration: how things in the game never seem to change. Their ground, The Valley was a nice big stadium but was closed in 1984 due to its failing to meet the necessary health and safety standards of the time and we moved to a ground share with Crystal Palace at Selhurst Park. This was tough on the players and supporters but for the coaching staff, we had to simply carry on regardless. It wasn't like being homeless but having your own ground is obviously something that you miss. Palace fans would often attend our games and boo the team just because it was Charlton. It did play on our minds and it wasn't a nice feeling.

We had a very young chairman called Mark Hulyer; a business man who it later transpired did not have the money that he professed to invest in to the club. He was being sued by a former chairman against bankruptcy.

Situated in the Second Division and winning promotion to the top division at one stage, we battled away and worked as hard as we could to keep the team progressing. One of the frustrations of being a manager or coach is seeing your players failing to implement what you have just told them to do during the half-time break. This is when your assistant is useful to sound off to; so that is why when you watch a game on television, the dug-outs are often scenes of fervent animation.

The fans were tolerant of the players and understood the financial instability. In the dressing room at half time Lennie had his say to his players and would then ask me if I wanted to contribute. I appreciated this and it cemented a good relationship between us. When you are in football, it isn't easy to keep the players focused on their game when there are myriad off-field concerns. You just have to make sure that you do your job and keep things going; it really is the only way to do it. Me and Lennie got on well and when you think of all the trouble we were in at the football club, money-wise, we did very well there.

Both of us went on to manage at Cardiff City on separate occasions and brought success to the club; following on from my period with them, Lennie subsequently went there as the new Director of Football in January 2002 and got them promoted to Division 2 at the close of the 2002/03 season. They also won the FA Wales Cup at the close of the 2001/02 season. He was most-recently working with Bristol Rovers after leaving the demanding south Wales club at the close of the 2004/05 season. I will talk more about my time at Cardiff in some detail in a later chapter. We retuned to the Bluebirds as opposing managers for a special match to open its new Cardiff City stadium on 4 July 2009. The stadium is situated across the road from the old Ninian Park ground and I was in charge of the 'Eddie May All Stars' against the 'Lennie Lawrence All Stars' with players selected from both our periods in charge featured in our respected first XI. Cut backs at Charlton eventually saw me leave after I was offered a role coaching the reserves. Lennie was put in a compromising position but by declining the offer there was no animosity and I left amicably enough.

After my departure from Charlton Athletic I continued to watch games up until a football agent contacted me with an offer of an interesting coaching position. It was to work for a club called Al Nahada in a country called Qatar, which is a part of the United Arab Emirates.

It would be whilst working here that I would get to become great pals with Len Ashurst, an association that would later bring me great success.

I spent a season at Al Nahada in a country where summertime temperatures would reach fifty degrees. My time there was a period from which I achieved nothing. We finished our campaign in a mid-table position and I didn't feel that I was improving the team or players. It was all to do with their beliefs and attitudes.

I would get so frustrated (as Len would also, in his job there). The team would come in at half time and I would be seething: ready to tell them exactly what I thought. A player that I had at Cardiff, Roger Gibbins, later my assistant there, has since labeled my managerial style as vocal but what can you do when the players come in and start praying? The situation there drove me mad as I could not express myself. It's different now because Qatar and Dubai, situated in the same region, are both very commercial: everything is about money. Fifa awarded the country the 2020 World Cup and there is even talk that the tournament will not be staged in the traditional summer months due to the high humidity. Perhaps England might stand a decent chance of winning it if its players aren't jaded after completing a long season. The club players in Qatar always gave me the impression that they were not playing to the best of their abilities. They never believed in themselves. It was a job at which I was going nowhere. I was getting paid but for the first time in my career, I felt that I was achieving nothing, that I was getting money for old rope. It was a job but also felt a bit like a holiday.

By 1987 I was off on my travels again and my next job was in all places, Iceland. Len Ashurst and I had kept in touch and I was to later hear from him with an offer of a job back in the UK but for now, I was the head coach at a club called KS Sigulfjord. I flew over to Reykjavik and immediately I got on well with the people at the club, a very family-orientated one and Iceland was a beautiful country to live in. It is a clean place, expensive but with fabulously clear air. I enjoyed my time there and if I am entirely truthful, it was a good place to be to maintain my CV in anticipation of a better job elsewhere. I was there for about a year and a half and left KS in a mid-table position. The domestic league there is split in to three divisions and nowadays they play in the Second and sometime after went on to be Icelandic Champions in 2004, after previously being so in 1989.

When I got a post there, my first day was a real culture or rather, nature shock. Experiencing my first morning there, I made way out of the house allocated to me only to find myself waist-high in snow. I really had no idea what to expect. Fans of the game out there would travel in small planes to attend matches and it was the same for me and my team. The Icelandic pilots were hugely skillful in dealing with the extreme weather and complex topography of the area and guiding their twenty-seater planes. The village that I was based in was within a basin and all around were mountains. Depending upon the wind, the plane would have to turn on its side to manoeuvre its way in. If we hit any mist, we would have to come underneath it and fly around the mountains to get back. It was really hazardous and a terrifying way for us to travel.

In Iceland, the local players definitely enjoyed a good punch-up after a drink and the place proved to be a bit of a battleground. In neighbouring Norway, the chairman was concerned for Marlene's welfare.

"Is he good to you?" He asked her.

"Because he seems a very aggressive man. We here are used to conversing about the outcome, so everyone's opinions are taken in to account."

She regarded them as being true socialists but with loads of money. One of my teams included twins who proved to be quite a handful. Marlene says that at every club I have been involved with, there has been a great deal of respect by my players but probably an equal amount of fear instilled in them. In Iceland, we enjoyed good crowds. The capital was a couple of hours away by fast boat but most of the fishing villages had football teams and the whole place would go to watch their team play. Games usually went ahead even in spite of the snow; this was possible due to the pitches sitting on a cinder base. If there was snow around or a thaw in process, we would play on this surface regardless of the ground still being frozen underneath. Players were primarily local lads with the bigger clubs including some foreign players in their sides.

From a football point of view, there is not a great deal of difference in the Scandinavian countries. Support-wise, the Icelandic League and Norwegian league had a lot of families attending the matches. It was to Tornado FC in Raudeberg, Norway that I next moved to in 1989 after being in the former country from 1987 onwards. Tony Knapp, a well-known former centre half at Leicester City was living in Norway some years later and mentioned to me that Tornado was looking for a new coach and so he mentioned me to them. I was given the position of head coach and the team advanced to being runners-up in the domestic league in 1990. We had a decent chairman and it was a relaxed environment within which to work.

When I was briefly working over there Marlene and I got invited by a friend of the chairman's for a weekend away at an exclusive island retreat. To get there, we had to travel by boat as the destination was some way out. We were told that we would be picked up and both of us imagined that it would be via a traditional fishing boat-type thing but when the time came to go; it was a fantastic, high-tech speed boat that arrived. The Norwegian fishermen are very rich and not at all as you might imagine.

Everyone had an enjoyable evening drinking and dancing until it was time to go back. It was the early hours and so pitch black. Returning was a terrifying experience as our vessel hit some rocks. A 'Mayday' signal was sent out and when the crew began bailing water, both me and Marlene were pretty worried. All on board were allocated life jackets but by the time that I was given mine, all that remained was a child-sized one which I could barely get on. The boat was now drifting and the danger apparent to us all. Others said to us that they usually didn't come out on to the sea as they had all lost friends and family in the past and feared it. You can imagine how we reacted upon hearing that. Marlene had recently bought me an expensive Jaeger jacket which she demanded that I take off in case it got ruined: she always got her priorities right, that one. I said to her, "If we go down, can I stick with you, as you're a good swimmer?" She politely declined and muttered something about this not being the time for the Musketeer spirit.

A huge boat eventually arrived and wound our boat up safely in a most efficient manner and thankfully, we were okay. With all of us wrapped up in thick blankets and drinking hot chocolate, if I'd have had my way, we would have jumped over board earlier and chanced our arm that way. Marlene had responded by saying that we were in the middle of the North Sea and wouldn't last five minutes in the cold water. In actuality, one of the guy's that rescued us said that we probably would have made it to ten minutes.

Another board member at the same club later offered us the use of a holiday home on the same island. Despite it having its own exclusive beach, I refused as I didn't want to return there. Marlene persuaded me to accept this rare opportunity to stay in such a luxurious home and so I agreed. We took a taxi boat there and met some lovely people and both enjoyed the break. Not having any sea legs or liking for the water especially, when we were due to leave the island there was some initial confusion as to which of the two jetties we should go to. I saw that there was already a boat moored at one of them and so we dashed towards it.

Someone then brought a person on a stretcher onboard and I offered him a cup of tea from the flask that Marlene had prepared earlier.

"He's very rude, him, isn't he?" I said to her.

"What's the matter with him, then?" I asked one of the guys there.

"He's dead." Came the reply. "You're on the hospital boat."

The Norwegians enjoy entertaining at home and are fortunate enough to live in beautiful, natural surroundings. Houses in the area where I stayed were stunning to look at too. Having been brought up in London, there is not a lot that I can do with nature, it distresses, confuses and throws me completely. I have to confess, I went to all these different countries purely for the football as the game was all I was really focusing upon.

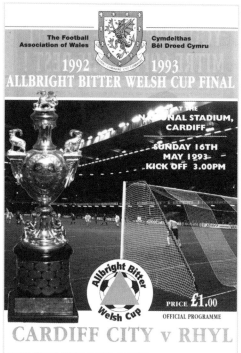

Above: Success came when I joined Cardiff City as a coach and we completed the League and Welsh Cup 'double' during the 1992/93 season. The latter thanks to a 5-0 thrashing of Rhyl at the National Stadium, Cardiff.

Left: A Welsh Cup Final winner again, only this time as a coach, after I had won the trophy as a player with Wrexham.

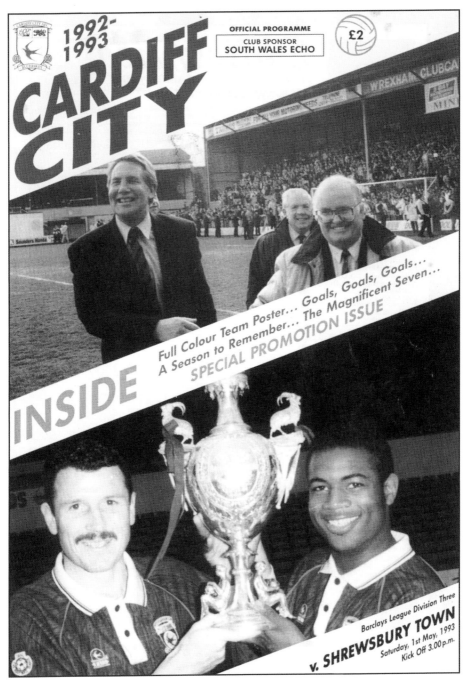

Above: Welsh Cup winners and promotion in that amazing season.

7
EDDIE MAY'S BARMY ARMY

I arrived at Ninian Park, the original home of Cardiff City FC, as assistant to manager Len Ashurst, in October 1990. We had developed a friendship back in 1986 when both of us were involved in football in the Middle East. I was the coach at Al Nahda and our teams would train in the late afternoon due to the heat and soon afterwards the two of us would meet up in a local café to discuss all-things football. Our location was quite extreme, with cities in built up areas sandwiched by desert. Len and I lived about a half hour distance from each other so it was easy to hook up.

In his day, Len made more than four hundred appearances as a Sunderland defender, still a record I believe, which earned him the nickname of 'Lenny the Lion' for his gritty determination. His most successful time as a manger was clearly with Newport County from 1978-82 when they won promotion, the Welsh Cup and reached the quarter finals of the European Cup Winners' Cup. They had some handy players such as John Aldridge, Tommy Tynan and Nigel Vaughan in their team then. He is a straight-talking man, thorough and a good coach. Whilst I remained in Qatar, Len returned to the UK sooner than I did to take charge at Cardiff in late-August 1989 and remained there through to May 1991, which was when I took over in early August. It was the second of his two tenures with the Bluebirds, his first having been from March 1982 to March 1984.

By the time I was offered the job training the kids at Cardiff, I was over in Norway where I was working with FC Tornado. I returned to London to make the necessary arrangements and to meet the City team who happened to be playing a cup game at Portsmouth. I watched the match and went back to Wales with them and it all began from there. I met everyone again at Ninian and soon heard rumours that the club were struggling financially. I have to say that I was unaware of their plight which as it turned out was pretty dire even back in the 1980s with debts of three million pounds by 1985.

Tony Clemo was the chairman then and he did say that he was hoping to bring someone in that would help the club and that person turned out to be a man called Rick Wright: more about him later. Tony came to the City back in the mid-1979s as part of a consortium that took over the club. By 1986 he had stepped up as Chairman but things between them soured eventually.

When I arrived back in Wales, I stayed at a guest house in Cardiff called the

Ty Gwyn. It was run by a certain lady called Marlene Raybould, of whom you have already heard, and pretty soon, she and I became close. Her place was then the base for trialists or those that City was interested in signing. It was a handy location as it was right near the city centre and not very far from the ground.

Marlene ran a very strict ship. None of the players that stayed there were allowed to bring anyone back and any adult material was not tolerated at all. One of them, Neil Matthews, was usually coerced in to asking if they could watch a dirty video but she wasn't having any of it.

They said to her, "Well what are we going to do in the evenings?"

"We're going to play Scrabble." Came her unexpected reply.

Out came the board and pretty soon everyone was loving it. We used to mess about a lot and some of the spelling was terrible. Lads such as Nathan Blake and Eddie Newton would demonstrate their Break dancing prowess in the lounge whilst Cohen Griffith virtually lived there too. He later got married and moved into his own house. The other Eddie remained in football after his playing days and was recently a head coach with West Bromwich Albion. Ed came to us on loan from Chelsea and subsequently returned there.

My first meeting with Marlene was typical of how things would go on between us. I arrived at her guest house only to find a note informing me to let myself in. I did so and after watching television for about a half-hour, I heard a voice say "Hello" followed by a vision appearing with red, spiky hair and wearing Andy Pandy-styled dungarees. She has since said that this was not my usual idea of how a woman dressed back then. At the time, Marlene and her husband were separated and he actually phoned her to warn her of my unruly reputation. "I took a few looks," she remembers, "and thought if this guy is a heavy drinker, then he could take my house apart. But I did notice that with the players Eddie was their natural boss." She said recently. "I think that was very evident from the word go. He was very much a man's man. And that was why it worked so well: they used to have fun together but they also worked hard together. It was a combination of the two and was almost like the Army."

A dressing room at a football club is not a place to be when the pressure is on. There are always confrontations and slanging matches between players and staff; people face up to each other because they care. At Cardiff, players such as Phil Stant and others would despair at being on the end of my dressing room blasts and 'Stanty' has since stated that I was a pretty gruesome sight when vexed. In my defence, I would state that I only ever came down on people when

I felt that they had done something wrong. Back at Wrexham when I was a player, our manager John Neal never used to rant and rave, unlike me. He would say, "What do you expect if we aren't passing the ball...if we aren't getting tight on people?" John was very practical with what he said to his players and he knew that he had people like me and Arfon Griffiths on the pitch who could handle the situation. We could deal with any problems should they arise. He was a quiet man that never ripped into his players.

I think that the days of frightening players are now long gone. You never hear of a fracas in the dressing room nowadays. Players are on good money and they have to accept things, up to a point, obviously. The best way to address any issues is to get a player to come into your office and deal with concerns privately. I used to have a go at one or two of them about their performance but if I had an issue about anything else, I would get them in my office. People like Paul Ramsey, Stant, Robbie James and Carl Dale, to a point, would do my job for me: the same principal applied at Wrexham. That's why we enjoyed success at both clubs. We would swear at each other, as players are wont to do; that's normal. In between, with Jock Wallace at Leicester City, I would watch him all the time: how he handled a player, any given situation and so forth and store it in my data bank.

I used to laugh at Marlene, as she may not have known anything about football but she was a good judge of character. All the differing personalities had to fit in to their roles on the pitch and (I would describe it like a human cake mix: it's getting the different ingredients working together). The football world can often be a self-centred environment and its all about ego. We work off adrenaline. The lads that came to the guesthouse were often very outgoing and most of us would socialise by going down to the wine bar in Cardiff Bay. It was like a family. I found that I could live in the same place as some of them quite easily.

For the 1989/90 season, with Len Ashurst at the helm, Rick Wright was their new chairman and had managed to remove a fair amount of debt accumulated prior to his arrival. Rick was a charismatic man and had made his money as the owner of the old Butlins aka Majestic holiday camp on Barry Island, near Cardiff. Comedy fans will know the surrounding area as a location for the recent smash BBC series Gavin and Stacey.

By the end of the 1990/91 season, with the club in Division Four, this was to be remembered as 'dour and unremarkable'. And in May 1991, Len was sacked (and subsequently took up a managerial role at his beloved Sunderland). By then I had been with Cardiff just over eight months after replacing Bobby Smith, a former Wrexham player, as coach back in October of the year before. The club finished in thirteenth position in Division Four, in the same division as my old club, Wrexham.

Tony Clemo, a man who loved Cardiff City, asked me if I wanted to take over the team and I agreed. In the beginning I was the club coach and after my first season Rick Wright subsequently made things more formal and gave me the manager's job. I was sad to see Len leave Cardiff as it wasn't a question of taking his job as I told him that I had been made an offer. All he said was, "Take it. It's not your doing (his departure). Take it."

'IT'S MAY TIME FOR THE CITY.'

SOUTH WALES ECHO HEADLINE, 11 JULY 1991.

I was now installed as the new head coach following the departure of Len Ashurst and my promotion from youth team boss. Rick Wright was now recognised as the club's 'financial controller' although Clemo still remained as the chairman and would do until 1992 when he was asked to stand down by Wright. A year before he was to sell his interest in the club for £200,000 to Rick who initially allowed him to stay on as Chairman. It is well-documented that in January of this year that they couldn't afford to pay the players/ staff wages and that the football club was only days from being wound up.

Rick informed the local press of his intention to keep me away from the small print over players' contracts and let me focus on team matters. He was an adept marketing man and said to me that for this season he was going to introduce a sliding scale of admission prices to Ninian Park. Depending upon our position in Division Four, classifications of category A, B or C would be introduced and the cost of a ticket would be dependant on our league position. We all knew that if you are top, the crowd would pay anything to come and watch but if you were slipping down the league then obviously, less people would come. It was a good philosophy and people remarked to me that this was a clever idea that had not been done before. General admission to the beloved Bob Bank, officially titled the Popular Bank but never, ever called as such by the fans, was £3.00 as we opened our campaign on August 17 with a 1-2 defeat by Lincoln City. A crowd of 5,137 was there that day with Chris Pike getting our goal via a penalty. The figure might seem low but at the time it was an improvement upon all crowd admissions from the home fixtures of the previous season.

Optimism was brimming all around the club with the players seemingly open to the new possibilities for the coming season. We just missed the play-offs, finishing the run-in at ninth position. Along the way we put eight goals past Wrexham across our two league meetings and hitting the goals for me were Carl Dale and Chris Pike, who collectively, struck forty three times in the league. 'Pikey' netted two hat-tricks this season also.

I think that we did quite well that initial campaign and proved consistent in our performances. It was important for me to make an impression on the chairman as I was on trial as a manager. We hadn't spent any money because he was looking at me to see what I could do and if I was able to absorb the pressure, deal with the players, the press and everything else. It really was a case of making the most of what I had there: which can be mightily difficult as sometimes there are players that you cannot improve. The grandstand got a new roof and seating was incorporated on the upper section of the Bob Bank.

We won the Welsh Cup that season with a victory over Hednesford Town at the National Stadium, in May, thanks to a Dale winner. It was our first appearance in a final there and the win was enjoyed by an attendance of 11,000. A club like Cardiff was always expected to win the Welsh Cup but I would say that your side still has to physically beat the teams, first of all. Often the smaller teams would be pumped up for the fixtures and it was sometimes tough to break them down.

A smashing character at the club was a guy called Harry Parsons, or 'H' as he was known. Although given the official job title of kit man, he was a great asset to Cardiff City as he would put his hand to anything including keeping the trainees on their toes.

Overall attendances at Ninian Park totaled 227,828 with cracking gates coming against the likes of Swansea City, Crewe Alexandra, York City, Shrewsbury Town, Wrexham, Lincoln City and Barnet, most notably. Away gates featuring City came in at 105,622 [not including the Welsh Cup Final which was staged at the neutral National Stadium, Cardiff].

THE 1992/ 1993 SEASON: A SEASON TO REMEMBER

After my endeavours in a Wrexham shirt in the European Cup Winners' Cup in the 1970s, here I was at the commencement of this new season as the latest Cardiff coach. I was back in the same competition due to our Welsh Cup final success in May 1992. In our opening game, we faced Austrian side Baumit Admira Wacker in a first round, first leg fixture at Ninian Park on 16 September 1992. City were ninth in Division Three at that time after seven league fixtures had reaped only a trio of wins. Back then, clubs were only allowed to field a total of three foreign players and this I feel influenced the eventual outcome for us. A mid-week tie ended in a 1-1 draw seen by a crowd of just over 9,500; some of whom no doubt included native Austrians who were allowed free admission thanks to another of those publicity ideas from our chairman. Our opponents qualified for the tournament thanks to reaching the Austrian Super Cup back in July 1991 whilst Cardiff had last seen European action in the 1989/90 season. Baumit joined the list of teams that had matched themselves against the Bluebirds since the 1960s, with others including Standard Liege, Hamburg, Sporting Lisbon and Dynamo Tbilisi.

I had my former Swans captain Robbie James back from injury for the second leg tie our captain, the youngster Jason Perry, was unavailable. The return match did not go well for Cardiff and we were beaten 2-0 at Wacka's Substandt ground in front of a crowd less than half that had seen the first tie. None of our strike force of Pike, Dale or Blake could affect the result. Fans might ask why we never did very well in such European encounters but you have to remember that in Wales, you had to win the Welsh Cup, not a national cup, to qualify for the European Cup Winners' Cup. It was feasible to see teams such as Barry Town, Cardiff or Maesteg winning it and competing against the likes of Real Madrid. Teams like that are the best in their respective countries and usually in their top flight, domestically. Whereas our teams did not always do so: think Wrexham, Cardiff and Newport County. So they do not always possess the best players, obviously. You knew that you were competing against better players too. Admira might have beaten us 3-2 over the two games but they too flopped, being eliminated by Belgian side Royal Antwerp in the next round.

Our opening league encounter came against Darlington in August and although it failed to produce any goals, nearly 9,000 fans turned out to support us for the start of this new campaign. A Season ticket for the Bob Bank cost £100 and would prove to be of tremendous value to those that splashed out on one. This campaign I found that I had to use a variety of striking options due to a bucket-full of injuries. Just as it always seems to be, Cardiff only had a small squad of players to choose from and this year was no different.

Cohen Griffiths had the knack of scoring winners for us and he seized his opportunity upon being selected for the first team getting us points on the board from victories against Walsall, Rochdale and Gillingham. Cohen was in a team that included Phil Stant, Dale and big Chris Pike who nabbed half-dozen goals across as many consecutive home games this season. Dale had been hitting the net since his non-league days with Bangor City. Attendances continued to be pretty strong too, with 10,411 attending our Boxing Day match with York City which ended 3-3.

Players such as Damon Searle, James, Perry, Derek Brazil, Gavin Ward and Nathan Blake all played more than 40 times during a campaign which saw eight of our goals coming from penalties. Overall attendances that season at home totaled 227,828 with cracking gates coming against Swansea City, Crewe, York, Shrewsbury, Wrexham, Lincoln City and Barnet, most notably. Away gates featuring City came in at 105,622 [not including the Welsh Cup Final which was staged at the National Stadium, Cardiff].

Advancing on into the season, Kevin Ratcliffe came to the club. He was coming to the end of his career and was signed on a game-by-game basis. Incredibly, even though he was a recent European Cup Winners' Cup and FA Cup winner with Everton, and their captain, he was let go by them after making three hundred and fifty nine appearances. Rats' was regarded by fellow Welsh international team mate Mickey Thomas as one of the best defenders in the world during his playing days. 'Noddy' had returned as a Wrexham player in his mid-30s and rejoined his old mate Joey Jones when Cardiff played them in the 1991/92 season. As a Cardiff man, my path with Wrexham crossed regularly, with mixed results. For example, when my former team mates Joey and Mickey played on a Friday night encounter at our place in December '92, they took away a 1-2 win but on another occasion, we beat them 0-2 at the Racecourse.

But back to Kevin, he made his debut for us against Carlisle United, away in the following January, a 2-1 win for his new club and he scored the winner thanks to a rare header! At half time I had let rip into our keeper whose mistake had led to us conceding as the first forty five minutes came to a close. 'Rats' goal came from a cross, I remember. His versatility was such that he could play in any position in the back four and when I brought him in, others in the team were pleased that I had done so as the defence had been struggling. Kevin now works as a match summariser for Radio Wales.

By January '93 Cardiff had gone on an extensive run of games without defeat and by mid-March it totaled eleven. Some healthy results had been gathered against Torquay United, 4-0 at Ninian Park in February and a 2-4 away win at Colchester United in March.

An important aspect of my job would be to watch prospective players two or three times before trying to buy them. Rick Wright had taken a chance in appointing me because I had no managerial or league experience at the time and so I wanted to do well for him this season. I was desperate not to fail. When I got to deal with him on a daily basis, he would often say things but then change his mind. He would tell me that he wasn't prepared to spend x amount of money but would then come back to me a week later asking me to repeat what I had said regarding a prospective signing. An early example of our professional relationship could be defined in the following scenario. I would ask him if I could have so-and-so on loan and this is the case of Carl Dale, I went to his then-club Chester after having reports back about his potential. I watched him a few times and was suitably impressed. They told me that they wanted £110,000 for him and so I went to Rick and told him that Carl was a goal scorer and would be a big asset to Cardiff. My chairman told me to go and offer them £50,000 to which I was flabbergasted.

"I can't do that!" Came my response. "He's keeping them in the division. The guy scores for nothing." Henry MacNally was the Chester chairman and after watching Dale in another game I went in to his office and had a chat.

"Fucking fifty grand! Don't be silly, Eddie. I've been offered fucking eighty!"

He could not stop laughing! I said if they gave him to us on loan then I could demonstrate his talents to Rick and guarantee that we would sign Dale. Mac held firm at first but did ask his board and they agreed to the offer, so long as we could put some money up front in good faith, then the deal was on. We later did so and Carl went on to set Ninian Park on fire. Everybody took to him there and the chairman came in beaming one day and told me to sign him, no matter what. Carl was a terrace hero and a favourite at Cardiff straight away. He was that kind of player; exciting and quick, had two good feet and was great in the air for a small guy. The fans, as I say, took to him immediately and he was a super signing for me: a great professional. In all he played some two hundred and fifty three games for us and hit ninety four goals.

Wright wasn't an awkward person to get on with: it was a question of trying to convince him about my ideas as he was not what I would call a football man. He later acknowledged publicly that we had learnt about business and football via an exchange of our obvious individual aptitudes.

In this my second season in charge, he gave me more authority and I had convinced him that I was a hard worker and that things were coming together well. As I have already mentioned, he owned a thriving holiday camp on Barry Island and I think that he took over the club for the people of Barry. He wanted it to be known that he pulled Cardiff City Football Club out of the mire and indeed, he did clear debts upon his arrival. I think a lot of people were thankful when he came to Cardiff: I certainly was as he gave me my break into management. He knew what he wanted to achieve and said to me, "If you want money, I'll give you money but I want success."

Even now, I still ponder on the question that if he had stayed with us just what more could we have achieved together? I certainly believed that there was more to come, but of course, that was never to be. We were getting great home gates and there was a lot of money coming in to the club. Rick was paying the wages for us all to do a job: if you did it well, he would be prepared to back you. When it came about that he was later going to leave, I said to him that he would not but he was adamant. In this season he had made it public that he was standing to make a £1.5m return on an outlay of £1m if we got promotion; so no pressure there then!

My first signing for the club was Paul Ramsey who I would stake my life on. I had worked with him when he was part of the youth team at Leicester City where I brought him through and he advanced to being club captain. By the time he came to us Paul had played close to 300 games for Leicester and had been capped at international level by Northern Ireland. It was during the 1989/90 season that Leicester was struggling and they narrowly missed relegation to Division Three for what would have been the first time. Frontline changes were rife at Filbert Street and when Brian Little came in as the new manager, he said that he would offer Paul a new contract but they couldn't agree terms. Paul felt that his time as a player should be properly acknowledged by an improved contract but things just didn't work out and no deal was struck.

That was where Cardiff City came in and we spoke on the phone a number of times, bashing out terms, prior to his eventual signing for the Bluebirds. Myself and the chairman said exactly what we were expecting from Paul when he was at the club and therefore, I knew him and what he could do for us by the time I brought him to Cardiff for the 1991/92 season.

Now working in outside catering and recovering from knee surgery, Paul recalls his reasons for coming to the south Wales club. "As a young lad, I liked what Eddie had to say about the game and liked their chairman too. I had heard about how passionate the City fans are and how they want you to feel about playing for them. So I took up the challenge and loved my time there. Eddie's approach was more considered at Cardiff than back at Leicester as he was now dealing with a mature type of player. He still told people what he thought but his man-management skills had changed. When he was in the changing room,

Eddie would really let you know exactly what he thought of your performance. Some of the weaker players struggled with this but often he would reassure them afterwards with an arm around the shoulder. But football is a tough old business."

Wright made quite an impression on everyone that he met: good or bad and Paul remembers his initial thoughts about him. "He was a strong man that you would not choose to cross. He was fair to the players and paid decent salaries whilst also offering good bonuses for success on the pitch." Like me, Paul too thinks that Rick should have changed his mind about leaving the club after a two year period, and built upon the success garnered on the pitch by the double-winning side. "He was honest with me." recounts the Derry-born play maker.

Speaking of the chairman, across my life in football, I have obviously dealt with many of them and not all have proved to be people that you would necessarily want to be involved with. They have to be very strong, dogmatic personalities and at Cardiff, we certainly had one of those. Rick didn't create a good impression in everyone that he met; often quite the opposite in fact. Marlene had quite an uncomfortable introduction to him which she remembers to this day. "He and Eddie were going to Geneva for the European Cup Winners' Cup draw and Rick asked me how I felt about it. I replied that it was very nice for him. "Yes." He replied. "I think it's very nice for me too. Because with Eddie's looks and my money we can pull all the girls with big tits." She realised that he wanted to see her response but remained unabashed. "Mr Wright," she replied, "Eddie wouldn't need your money to pull anything."

Like Paul Ramsey, Carl Dale was exactly the same in that sense. I was lucky because I had this theory that if I was going to sign somebody, they could be the best player in the world but they had to be a good character too. Paul Millar, another lad from Ireland came to City from Port Vale via a 60k transfer fee and could play in either mid field or up front. The fans didn't quite take to him as he was a strong player, very robust. A 100% professional in training, his debut for the Bluebirds came in a Rumbelows Cup match back in August 1991 which we won 3-2. Then I signed Phil Stant, which was the icing on the cake. He scored goals regularly, wherever he went. Some people said to me that perhaps he had been to too many clubs in his career but my response was that was because he scored goals at whichever club he was at. 'Stanty' proved to be a very important signing for me: a real tough guy. Whenever I saw him play he would give opponents so many problems. Phil was not the quickest but he had this skill of gliding in to space well. He had very long strides but you never got the impression that he was flat out when he was running. His hard work was appreciated by his team mates. He could drift off defenders beautifully too. Combined with Dale, Phil was a great foil for the former who had the ability to spin and leave people standing with his pace. As a duo, I regard these two as my strongest pairing up front in the Cardiff front line. All these players were great characters who did their job well: Dale & Stant hitting the goals and Ramsey creating and organising things in the midfield. I also signed former Swansea hero Robbie James from Bradford who by then had featured in more than 700 first team games. I had played with him when he was a teenager back at the Vetch Field when I was coming to the end of my playing career. He was as hard as nails, even then. Robbie could use both feet and I managed to bring him to Cardiff for £40,000: peanuts for a player of his quality. So with these four, either in the dressing room or on the training ground, any one of them would pull people in line if anybody was acting inappropriately. They would quickly put them straight and that's what you want as a manager: men who could do this when necessary. That's the way I worked.

Domestically, we went on to win the new Division Three as Champions, taking care of most of the teams in that same league as the season progressed. This campaign, one I will always remember, saw one hundred and nine goals scored by the team: seventy five and thirty four league and cup goals respectively, across fifty six games [forty two league fixtures and the rest being F.A Cup Coca Cola Cup, Autoglass Trophy, European Cup Winners' Cup & Welsh Cup games]. Leading my table of goal scorers would be Carl Dale on twenty nine, Phil Stant on eighteen; including hat-tricks against Maesteg Park Athletic and Rhyl and Nathan Blake on fourteen.

However, embarrassment did come in the form of an FA Cup upset in front of our own home fans thanks to a 2-3 defeat to Bath City in November. This in spite of two recent league wins against Colchester United and Scunthorpe United. Many of the players have since stated that this was the catalyst for us to push on and improve that season and I would like to think it was, as results definitely picked up. That defeat was a blip. It was a case of the underdog having its day, something which I was fully aware of from back in my playing days with Wrexham: such is the magic of the FA Cup. Bath were then in the Conference league and were subsequently knocked-out in the next round by Northampton after a replay. However, I have to say that all at the club were embarrassed after the result and we made sure that it wasn't going to be repeated. Professionally, we pushed on in the league and went on to win many games. After the Christmas festive fixtures 'Blakey' aptly declared that we were the side to beat and by March Cardiff had taken thirty seven points out of a possible thirty nine.

Ominously, Wright told the local Western Mail newspaper in April that, "... we are going nowhere next season unless the club is sold or I am given the financial backing required." At one point in 1993 Rick made it public that he had 'given' the club to 8,500 children City fans in an attempt to avoid occurring further debts or I don't know what. It was a bizarre idea but the press lapped it up.

On the pitch, a pivotal result saw my return to Wrexham at the Racecourse in late-April where we won 2-0 and I received a warm welcome from the home fans. It was a hugely important win and the press had been promoting it as such throughout the build up to the match. The all-ticket encounter was probably Cardiff's finest performance all season and it was a day to remember for everyone, players and fans alike, as in unison, an estimated 4,000 Cardiff fans did the infamous 'Ayatollah' gesture. I remember doing an interview where I stressed my loyalties towards my present club even though I still had a tremendous fondness for Wrexham. At one stage in the season, we had amassed thirty four points from twenty outings.

Promotion had been sealed by the time of the final match of the domestic season on May 8, a 0-3 away win against Scunthorpe in front of 7,407 at Glanford Park. The win made us go up as champions, the first time Cardiff had been such in forty six years. Cardiff were at the time of kick-off, one point ahead of Barnet and three ahead of Wrexham, whilst 'Scunny' were tenth from bottom. We had already met at our place back in October, where we ran out winners by 3-0. An exuberant but friendly pitch invasion by City fans ensued.

Our final home game had seen a terrific 17,253 there to endure a hard-fought 2-1 win against Shrewsbury Town. As would be the case in the final fixture to come at Scunthorpe, our fans again showed their joy by racing on to the pitch at full time. A little over sixteen thousand, the best in the division, had previously attended the top-of-the-table clash with Barnet at the end of March (we drew 1-1).

Meanwhile, with the club having already attained promotion, we swept aside Rhyl in the Welsh Cup final, thanks to an excellent 5-0 drubbing at the National Stadium on May 16th. It rounded off an excellent season and was City's twenty first Welsh Cup Final appearance win. We were presented with the championship trophy before kick-off at the National Stadium in Cardiff in front of a crowd of 16,433. The majority of which were City fans and they were to enjoy a whole-hearted routing of our opponents that Sunday afternoon. But little did they know of the turmoil going on off the pitch. I had to say to Phil Stant that if I selected him to play in the game then this would be his acknowledgement of not pursuing a bonus claim with the chairman. Stanty was furious with Rick but wasn't prepared to miss the day and all that it entailed. Fortunately for us, he hit a hat trick and we ran out 5-0 victors. Phil subsequently took his claim to the Football League and won the case much to the chagrin of our chairman. He very publically declared that the former soldier would never play for the club again. It transpired that this was not quite the case but Phil was returned to his former club Mansfield Town on loan and later sold to Bury.

We had performed well in the early rounds of the competition and had enjoyed a satisfying 2-1 aggregate defeat of Wrexham in the semi-final stage. The older fans at that club remembered me as a player and would come up to me after the games and offer their congratulations. We had a good record against Wrexham when I was at Cardiff but as far as I was concerned, I wanted to beat them as much as I could because that's the way I thought about it. I had a fantastic time there as a player and achieved a great deal. The Racecourse has a hall of fame which includes a mention of yours truly, something I am very proud of. The tribute celebrates the late-1960s/early-1970s playing era, arguably Wrexham's finest. After moving on from playing for Wrexham, in opposition, I always received a decent reception from them. Arfon Griffiths will tell you that I was and still am, well-thought of at the club.

Returning to the Welsh Cup, in an early encounter away at Caerau, we battered them 9-0 with a hat-trick from Nick Richardson and 4 from Carl Dale. In the final, as mentioned, Phil Stant nabbed a hat-trick. Born in Bolton, Stanty signed for Cardiff in December 1992. As he lived in Mansfield and travelled back home straight after every match, I would often allow him to train up there and sometimes have an extra day away, so long as he adhered to a rigid training schedule. A former SAS soldier, Phil had been engaged in active service during the Falklands conflict a few years earlier. He was a true fans' favourite amongst the Ninian Park faithful.

From a players perspective, Paul Ramsey succinctly summarises his time at Cardiff as thus, "In the first year, we struggled but by the second year things were good. Eddie had things well organised and the team had a great bunch of lads there. He was able to get his ideas through to the players and success came with us winning the League and cup double. I was made captain and enjoyed two of the best years of my playing career there. Robbie James, Roger Gibbins and I would socialise together whilst Eddie would occasionally have a drink with the lads before heading off to his own friends. But we all came together for the team and this was in no way a problem. It just seemed appropriate. Robbie was a lovely guy and knew a lot about the game too. Things went wrong at Cardiff when players were sold such as Nathan Blake. We lost momentum on the pitch but the fans were always behind us." At the season close, I had won two Barclays manager of the month awards, usually the kiss-of-death to recipients.

After the success of the 1992/93 season, I felt that I deserved a rest and so with Marlene, we went off to the luxurious Caribbean resort of St Lucia for an all-inclusive break. When we arrived, I was perturbed to see that we had been given a room which overlooked the garbage bins. We were paying a lot of money to stay there and I was furious. Half an hour or so later a group of guys came along and picked up the 'bins' which in actuality, were steel drums for a band!

Nottingham Forest and England star Stuart Pearce along with his wife were also staying at the hotel. I would see 'Psycho' out for his daily run and would say hello from the comfort of my sun lounger. Coincidentally, one of my Cardiff players, Jason Perry, now a radio match summariser, was also termed this by the City supporters. Emmerdale Farm actor Fraser Hines was another guest there too and he latched on to us and one day, challenged me to a game of tennis. I foolishly accepted but nearly killed myself as we played in the boiling, mid-day sun. Afterwards, I went back to the room and was left purple-faced after my on-court exertions.

Whilst at the resort, Marlene coerced me in to trying snorkeling for the first time too. I made the mistake of wearing the full outfit, flippers included, prior to getting down to the beach. Instead of tipping backwards into the water, as per the norm, I was attempting to go in head first. All the other guests were laughing, thinking that I was playing the fool but Marlene knew the truth. I am not at all at ease in the water. I did get in but had the fright of my life upon seeing a big shadow looming. I was only in shallow water but I thought that it was a shark: it later transpired that it was my own shadow that had spooked me. That marked the end of my snorkeling adventures.

Back to on-field matters, I selected playing stalwarts Damon Searle and Cohen Griffith for forty two of the forty six league fixtures across the 1993/94 season, whilst Jason Perry followed close behind on forty appearances. Nathan Blake would smash a hat-trick in a Ninian Park game against Stockport a day after Bonfire night; whilst Paul Millar did the same away at Brighton, in April.

Phil Stant totalled twenty two goals across the campaign whilst Nathan went on to nab a decent tally of seventeen.

Following our success at Cardiff City after the 1992/93 double-winning season, my name was mentioned for a succession of vacant managerial vacancies: Aberdeen, Bolton, Bristol City and Gillingham all showing interest in me. It was flattering but back then you couldn't have moved me from Ninian Park with a tank! You would think that I was in a safety zone after what had been achieved and our attendances were up into five figures but the whole thing went haywire. Rick Wright made a lot of money from Cardiff City Football Club and I said to him that we have got to build on what we have done now. He agreed. But I made it crystal clear that I meant we needed better players if we were going to improve as a team. Even supporters say to me now that Rick was crazy not to have taken on the challenge of moving the club forward. But it was as if he had made his money and that was it. When the Wright-owned, Majestic holiday camp went up for sale we all realised that it was over. There soon followed a huge upheaval at the club which had ramifications for everyone.

Indeed, the 1993/94 season in Division Two was a tricky one as there was great uncertainty amongst players and staff at the club. The opening away fixture saw Cardiff travel to Fulham on August 21. We came away with a brace from Nathan Blake resulting in a decent 3-1 win but the off-field events of that day marred things. Our chairman was publically scornful of those at this London club after crowd skirmishes between opposing fans in their family stand resulted in the game being stopped for twenty minutes. Attended by a gate of 5,696, somehow some of our supporters had got into one of their stands instead of the usual away space behind the goal. Mounted police moved on to the Craven Cottage pitch and I went to speak with our fans, to try and calm them down, as they would listen to me. Here's what I said about it in our club programme immediately following the fixture, "The trouble in the crowd could have been averted. That's not to condone anyone who caused trouble - there's a black mark against the club now and we just don't need that. There was a scuff, and I think Neil Kinnock (a big City fan) was spot on when he said there were about six people causing the problem and that there was no intervention. I don't want to make too much out of what happened, it's important that such incidents are seen in context. But it remains very disappointing that those few who do cause trouble give the club a bad name."

Former Match of the Day presenter Jimmy Hill was the Fulham chairman and he and I had not got on well since crossing paths at Charlton Athletic back in the mid-1980s when Jimmy was briefly involved with the 'Addicks' prior to becoming Fulham chairman in 1987. That incident had come about after he tried to tell me and then-manager Lennie Lawrence what we were doing wrong on the pitch. I said to Hill, "Who are you then? Do you work here?" He couldn't say much in response and we never spoke again but he obviously remembered me.

Cardiff had offered to take a group of their own stewards to police our fans but the offer was not accepted by the authorities at Fulham or the police authorities. Marlene and a friend had come to see the match and were in the Directors area that afternoon. Her friend had been expressing her support for us by yelling the team on but this did not go down well with the locals because at half-time they surround them and said that they had been making obscene gestures. That was just untrue. They were very intimidated by Hill and his cronies and were subsequently hidden away by a friendly tea lady who directed them the ladies where they locked themselves in to escape a very frightening situation. At the end of the match, there was no protection on offer for us and we took some abuse on the way back to the car. For a small minority of away fixtures the reputation of Cardiff fans preceded us but the treatment vetted out to Marlene and others that afternoon was atrocious.

As a manger Hill's only club was Coventry City in the 1960s. But like Marmite, you either love him or hate him as a personality: you can probably guess which camp I pitch up in. City's reputation both on and off the park was growing. Matters on the pitch saw us come away with a win in what was Robbie James' 775th appearance as a professional footballer. He was then thirty six years old. At full-time I applauded our diehard fans, as was my wont, only for Fulham boss Don Mackay to criticize me in the papers for doing so following the ruckus.

Just prior to that away game, we had beaten Leyton Orient 2-0 at home on the opening day of the season. Rick Wright caused a great deal of debate amongst fans at the time when he stated that if they bought £100,000 of season tickets this would allow for the return of Phil Stant. The two had fallen out over promised bonus payments to players and Rick made it clear that he did not want the Bob Bank favourite back. However, he stated in the press that if the fans demonstrated their desire to see his return, via their mass purchase, then he would allow it. To work it out, more than 700 season tickets would have been needed to be sold each at £140 and he only gave a three week deadline in which to achieve this! I had signed him for Cardiff in December 1992 and he hit nineteen goals in his first season with us. By the 1994/95 season, he had fifteen goals until he was loaned back to Mansfield Town. Later, Phil was sold to

Division Three side Bury for a bargain £65,000 in January '95. He had been ostracised by the chairman and had been training alone away from his team mates.

Thanks to winning the Welsh Cup, this season saw Cardiff again playing in the European Cup Winners' Cup. We got drawn away against another top Belgian side, Standard Liege, at their Stade de Solessin ground for a 15 September encounter. Liege were then managed by an old Euro foe of mine from my Wrexham playing days, Arie Haan, a former Ajax coach and a part of the prestigious Anderlecht side of the 1970s. Standard Liege had been Belgian Champions on eight previous occasions when we met them. More than a thousand City fans made their way to Belgium in anticipation of the fixture. Off the field, many arrests were recorded with hooligans said to have been planning to meet during the build up to this Wednesday-evening match. Liege had their own hooligan element known as the 'Hellsiders' and they were involved in skirmishes before kick-off.

Our own fans were confronted by armed riot police with random attacks occurring against anyone that happened to be in the way of their truncheons. I understand that the atmosphere was initially of a jovial nature, with fans enjoying a drink prior to the commencement of the game which soon saw Cardiff go 2-1 up just after the half hour. A crowd of 10,700 would see us eventually defeated 5-2. It was peaceful inside the ground but with riot police facing the Cardiff fans throughout the match. Also, in the return leg at Ninian Park, crowd trouble marred our 3-1 defeat in which Robbie James struck a brilliant twenty five yard shot. Significantly, that fixture marked the final occasion that a professional Welsh side would compete in the competition. Robbie eventually left Cardiff to join Barry Town. A little know fact about him was that although he had won promotions as a part of the terrific Swansea City sides of the late-1970s, it was as a Cardiff player that he received his first Champions medal.

Paul Ramsey and Kevin Ratcliffe both left the club as would a number of others. Roger Gibbins, who served City so well as a player, stepped up to coach and I later made him my assistant.

In January we met Middlesbrough in the FA Cup which resulted in a replay at their place following an enthralling 2-2 at Ninian on the eight of that month. They were managed by my old associate Lennie Lawrence and the second match saw a late winner, via a header, from an injured but still determined, Phil Stant to see us through. As our hectic league campaign progressed Cardiff were next drawn at home to Manchester City in the fourth round. We had already seen off

Enfield, Brentford and Boro, albeit thanks to a couple of replays and as per usual, we did our preparation in anticipation of meeting our First Division opponents. They had so much going for them, Manchester City: I was gob smacked at the thought of what I was going to say to motivate my players after seeing the blue side of Manchester perform so well. In spite of the match being shown live on television, a superb attendance totalling 20,486 were packed into Ninian on that Saturday afternoon where they saw local lad Nathan Blake hit a fantastic goal that secured our place in the next round.

Shortly after the hour, Blakey breezed past most of their defence and struck a curling left foot shot that left their keeper grasping at the air as the ball flashed into the net. It was a great shot and one that fans (and Nathan) still speak about to this day. Our own stopper, Mark Grew deserves some plaudits as he saved a penalty late on and I thought after the goal that maybe this was going to be our day.

Regrettably, we were to end our involvement with the competition with a disputed strike very late on in an away encounter at Luton Town. A massive 17,296 were in attendance at Kenilworth Road but we lost the game 2-1.

The Man City match proved hugely significant for both Cardiff City as a club and for both Nathan as a player and me as a boss, for different reasons. For the player, it put him in the shop window which took him away from City and for me; it showed that things were not as I would want as manager. Nathan had made his debut as a Cardiff player in March 1990 and played in defence and midfield before making a name for him self in the number ten shirt with forty goals in 164 outings. He was unsettled at the time of the cup game and in a pay dispute of sorts with the chairman. I believe that a player of Nathan's calibre didn't do justice for himself in terms of success as a footballer. He left us to join Dave Bassett's Sheffield United, which I didn't see as a step up for a lad of his calibre. Even when I occasionally see him now at Cardiff-related matches, he comes up to me and we hug each other. If you know Nathan, he is not prone to doing such things lightly. If you meet him today, the first thing you might think is that he is an arrogant so-and-so. I had a great relationship with him. Sometimes we would have words and at times Nathan would come in and if he had a personal problem, it would show in the way in which he trained. You would have to put your arm around him and ask what the matter was. When I was his boss at City, if I could do him a favour off the field, I would. I got on with him because I wouldn't stand for any of his nonsense. Sometimes I had to say to him, "Sit down, shut up and listen." If you spoke to Nathan on a man-to-man basis, you were okay. If you started shouting, it was a waste of time. On his day, he was the best player I had. He had everything: the hardest thing was to prove it to him. He could head, he could jump higher than anybody, had two good feet, would go into a tackle; there was nothing he could not do. The boy had everything. He just didn't put it in to practice. I don't think that he had enough ambition. You just have to look into his record for Wales. As an international player, Nathan Blake should have been a regular in the national team but if you look into his appearances total, he wasn't. Why?

Nathan was a fantastic player for Cardiff City and the money that took him to Sheffield, as I say, was nothing. He could do tremendous things on the pitch but I don't think he believed in himself. He went on to play for some big clubs. When I sold him to United I didn't like doing so as he was one of my players. His transfer gave me a hint that Rick Wright really was going to leave Cardiff, regardless Dave Bassett was a shrewd operator, and when he made the offer for Nathan I said that he should surely have added another 'zero' to the fee. I could not believe that Rick had accepted the deal as I honestly thought that he was going to decline their offer. I said, "You cannot sell him for that, surely? Hold out for more." Rick then replied that the fee was agreeable and the club would sell him. And that's when I realised that the club was going away from me. Cardiff was like a ship, when bits fall off, you know that you are going to sink. Other players like Stanty and Dale followed; these were top players, regular players. Paul Ramsey was my captain and he was forced out by a man that had previously brought success to City. This I did not understand. When we won the Championship and Welsh Cup, any chairman would be delighted: especially in only your second season in the game. But to then walk away from the football club was unbelievable to me: it was there and then that the whole thing started to fall apart. What followed was disastrous for the club and people won't forget Rick Wright for this reason: he brought Cardiff City to its knees. He made it but he also broke it.

Fans were coming up to me during all this and asking why we were selling various players but all I could say was that the chairman was probably trying to get some of his investment back.

The season was to be a tumultuous season for everybody at Cardiff after Rick called in to see me at Ninian Park one day and told me that he was selling the club and that a consortium was going to purchase it from him. He had said from the start that he only wanted to stay for a given period of time and he intended to stick to this pledge. They put their bid in motion but after a couple of weeks

I was still in charge of football matters until they informed me of their plans to install a new manager when they eventually took full control. I said okay but that they have to pay my contract up after which time I would leave. By the end of November 1994, after a miserable 0-2 defeat at home to Hull City on the twenty fifty of that same month I was dismissed as City boss even though my contract ran until August of the following year.

Cardiff-born Terry Yorath, himself a former Wales player and manager subsequently arrived to begrudgingly take charge for the Exeter City match on 29 November. This Auto Windscreens Shield away day encounter saw the team lost 1-0 away. A board meeting was declared for the following Monday after the above defeat. Terry had a column in the local paper at the time and commented upon my departure. "It has been sticky and in some parts has been messy. But what we all have to strive for is a better Cardiff City." However, I bet that what transpired was nothing like he imagined either! Results were mixed at the start of the season but we did enjoy decisive wins against Brighton, Bradford and a hat-trick performance from Phil Stant saw to Cambridge United too.

At a football club, conspiracy theories can bring a place to its knees. I know it happened to me at Ninian but not from the players but via the board room. A consortium consisting of marketing consultant Jim Cadman, Michael Boyce and others attempted on three occasions to buy City, installed former Wales player/ manager Yorath as manager but failed to come up with an agreeable package for the by-now Australia-based Wright. So he retained control and that's where I came back into the story. Writing in his autobiography Hard Man, Hard Knocks (Celluloid publishing, 2004), Yorath briefly details the frustration that the period caused him and also that he had not intended to be the manager. Terry, a past Swansea City manager stated that he had not wanted my job but did acknowledge that he had been somewhat naïve in getting embroiled in the whole business. Clearly the directors wanted me removed but he states that he voiced his belief that I should remain in the job and found the whole experience hugely frustrating. Terry ran the team matters after I left up until I received a phone call in early 1995 from Rick asking me to come back to Cardiff City Football Club.

I demanded that I would choose when I was to eventually leave, not him or anyone in the new consortium. I did this for a bit of self respect. He told me that Cadman and Bryce were remaining on the board but would have no say on most of the subsequent matters raised. I made it crystal clear to Rick that I would return to take care of the playing affairs until the end of the season. I could see that things were not going well on the field and I said to him that he had a cheek to ask me to come back. He had left me out on a limb but believed that the consortium did have the money and that he would have made it up to me.

"I know that I let you down." He offered. "I've learnt my lesson now with the wrong people."

I was still hesitant. "What's the point of me going back if you are not going to be there?" I replied.

We acknowledged that they had no hard cash to make this a reality and so he said that he wanted me to return.

"For how long?" I wondered.

Rick reaffirmed that regardless of anything else, he was going to leave at the end of the season even if he had to undersell the club. The Cadman-related consortium was one of a number that vied for prospective control of Cardiff, another involved a Midlands business man called Samesh Kumar, who was to play his part in the unfolding drama too.

After the debacle of my last few months with City, I had been keen to get straight back into football and that's when the Barry Town managerial post came about. Their chairman, Neil O'Halloran, an ex-City player from the late-1950s offered me the job there at their Jenner Park ground. So on January 26 1995 I was unveiled as the new Barry manager and that same month I returned to Ninian Park in a scouting capacity for Lennie Lawrence. He was then in charge at Bradford City, and I saw a goal-less encounter with Huddersfield.

I had unhappy recent associations involving Barry Town whilst at Cardiff and remembered the Welsh Cup Final of May 1994. What a terrible build-up that game was for me and the team; I had to hastily arrange for us to travel to the national stadium in taxis as the official coach failed to arrive at the hotel where we had been preparing (coincidentally, the Barry squad had also booked their pre-match at the same hotel!) I was furious when I learnt of the transport balls up and our fans were amazed to see the manner in which the players arrived for the game at the stadium.

A crowd gate totaling 14,130 were there to see us lose 2-1 in the capital city. That result shocked the football community in Wales.

The protracted sale of Cardiff City FC rumbled on as the team found themselves fourth from bottom of the table. Popular striker Phil Stant was not the only one frustrated with events at the club by the time talks took place on the sixteenth of that month. These flopped and Rick Wright returned. Still intent on selling his stake in the club, Cardiff City was now viewed by many as the 'laughing stock of league football'.

Often fans despair upon the arrival of a new boss whose last job or two proved ultimately unfruitful and the thought of them coming to their club hardly spurs them on. Barry Town was soon to become the first team in the area to become full-time professionals and the facilities at the club had been vastly upgraded when I took over. Major improvements were incorporated: an increase in seating capacity, a new hospitality complex, new dressing rooms, clubhouse and more. And similar to Newport County previously, Barry was well-known as a stopping-off point for former pros in the autumn of their playing careers. Mr Neil O'Halloran had been associated with them for some years and was known in the game as 'Mr Barry Town'. He asked me along and I enjoyed my brief spell there. I suggested bringing in a few established pros and so introduced my former Cardiff and Leicester player Paul Ramsey to bolster the team. When Terry Yorath was appointed manager at Cardiff this was when I went to Barry for the first time until the consortium at Ninian Park collapsed and Rick Wright initially asked me to return in January 1995. I looked upon my time at Welsh Cup holders Barry Town as a way of maintaining my involvement within football.

The end of the season was coming up and I knew that the post was not going to be long term. It was a question of a couple of months here and a couple there, whilst the club was in transition. Barry had the accolade of becoming the first club in their division to turn professional when I was there and I think doing this surprised them a little bit. People instantaneously expect far more of them. Neil became ill and said to me that he was going to sell the club (his wife would subsequently do so after his death) Nothing was final; be it at Cardiff or Barry and I saw out the end of the season and was done. Funnily enough, I can see Jenner Park from my home in the nearby area today.

Neil loved his football and you had to like him for that. He did all that he could for Barry whilst in charge but I still feel that the club could have advanced much more than it did. When I left, David Giles took over as manager. He and his brother, Paul, both former Cardiff City footballers, were also playing there when I made my entrance. It was these two who suggested getting me involved to Neil in the first place. The trouble with Barry was that if you won the title in their league, there was no where else to advance up to.

This was a big problem in my view.

"EDDIE IS BACK TO FINISH THE JOB HE STARTED."

SOUTH WALES ECHO.

That newspaper headline on Friday March 31st 1995 revealed that I was returning as Cardiff City manager. I came back only after having all of my outstanding salary paid to me and I made it clear that I would decide when I was leaving.

Also, that Rick would not make the rules about prospective signings and I wanted more money as I had to swallow my pride, in a public sense, in returning. By doing all this, I took back a bit of credibility. Immediately I set about informing the local media that I was coming back to manage the club until the close of the season in May. I knew that they would ask why this was but I was firm in stating that I knew exactly what was happening with regards to the consortium and take-over bids but that I returned for my own reasons alone. I had wanted to come back and thought that maybe there was a possibility that I would be retained even when new owners were eventually found.

Lots of changes at Ninian Park saw Terry Yorath depart and a bid from the Warburton consortium that he was a public figurehead for, collapse. Yorath checked out on the Thursday and I returned to take charge of team affairs immediately. My first game was a day later, a home fixture with my former Wrexham rivals, Chester.

Cardiff City 2 - Chester City 1, Saturday 1 April. Some inside the club didn't realize that I was returning and most of the 4,405 April Fools Day crowd had no idea either. But it was no joke: the chairman offered free admission to women and children which helped push up the gate from the 2,560 that had recently attended the Bradford home game; a 2-4 defeat. I received a warm welcome from the fans as Carl Dale put us 1-0 up by half-time. The win saw Cardiff positioned third from bottom in the Endsleigh Division Two and was only the fourth victory recorded all season. Leyton Orient and Chester City were below us in the table. In the crowd that afternoon were the Birmingham-based Kumar brothers and others from the remaining two groups seeking to take charge of the club. In spite of all the uncertainty I was pleased to have returned and happy that those that I regarded as being problematic had now been removed. Three separate bids had been presented to Mr. Wright and he had gone off to Australia to consider their various merits. On the field, we had a trio of home games coming up, the first of which was against fellow strugglers, Orient, three days later.

Cardiff City 2 - Leyton Orient 1, April 4. I have to say that the Bluebirds supporters really showed that they were behind the team by roaring us on to a valuable win after we had initially gone a goal down. Two late strikes from Anthony Bird won the match for us and we climbed up a place in the table. A Welsh Cup semi-final encounter with my old club Swansea City, was imminent but not before a league meeting with Rotherham.

Cardiff City 1 - Rotherham United 1, April 8. Rick offered free entry to under-sixteen's to watch a game within a division that would see 5 sides relegated by May. A gate of 6,412 saw the Guyana-born Cohen Griffith nab our only goal which meant that we dropped back down a position. Cardiff had managed to take seven out of nine points in recent games but was it all coming too late? When Rick did eventually cut his links with the club, it began an awkward time for me because I didn't know who was coming and going or if I would remain in the long term as manager. But I just had to get on with things.

Cardiff City 1 - Birmingham City 2, April 15. A testing away game at St.Andrews in front of a massive 17,455 saw defeat arrive for Cardiff via a 2-1 score line before we had to prepare rapidly for another home match.

Cardiff City 1 - Shrewsbury Town 2, April 17. Another strike from the boot of Anthony Bird put us at 1-1 but a goal a little after the hour mark resulted in seeing Cardiff perched at third from bottom after forty three games played. 'Birdy' had originally come in to the City set-up when I selected him for a game at Walsall in August 1992.

Brentford 2 - Cardiff City 0, 22 April. Defeat in front of an 8,268 crowd saw us relegated into Division Three by a team that was top of the division. The local press had termed my task of keeping City up as a 'mission impossible' but were they to be proved correct?

Cardiff City 0 - Bristol Rovers 1, 29 April. An 87th minute goal by our West Country visitors added to the list of defeats at home in a season within which the team won only five times in the league. We equalled the 1984/85 season tally when City was managed by former player Alan Durban (they got relegated too). On the positive front, we did record wins against Brighton & Hove Albion, Cambridge United, Wycombe Wanderers, Chester City and Leyton Orient.

Crewe Alexandra 0 - Cardiff City 0, 6 May. The final league game for me as manager was this away fixture attended by a gate totaling 4,382. We were already relegated by finishing twenty second in the table but out of interest, here's my team selection for that last game: Williams, Brazil, Searle, Wigg, Baddeley, Perry, Young, Richardson, Millar, Dale, Griffith.

Cardiff City 0 - Swansea City 0, 2 May In all, I was back in charge for eight games not including the above Albright Bitter Welsh Cup meetings with Swansea. We went in to this match with a 1-0 win from the first leg at the Vetch Field, in this return semi-final meeting. The Swans were then managed by a friend of mine, future Cardiff manager, Frank Burrows. They had beaten the Bluebirds 4-1 in a league match back in the previous March (before my return) and so the lads were keen to avenge that result when we met them in the Cup. An astounding thirty five yard strike by Paul 'Windy' Millar late on at the Vetch had given us an aggregate advantage in readiness for the oncoming return leg at Ninian Park. Victory came in a game that saw our regular keeper going off injured and his replacement saving a penalty. An attendance of 2,654 watched this spicy local derby.

The return fixture was to be my final match in charge of the team and I did an emotional farewell lap of honour at the end of the game to thank the fans. Cardiff progressed through to the final and saw an Arms Park meeting with Wrexham. It was the fourth consecutive final appearance for City and we had won a couple of those games previously. I remained in charge a little longer as the take-over was delayed but sadly, we lost 2-1, after coming back from 2-0 down. Results were underwhelming, what with so much going on around the club. The final league fixture, an away trip to Crewe (a 0-0) saw Cardiff finishing the season in 22nd position and consequently relegated. I left the club for the final time on May 22nd. I returned to manage at Barry Town once again from that September and left after a half-dozen games. All-in-all, a very trying period for me, professionally-speaking.

I had been in charge at Cardiff City since July 1991 and had always wanted to be a club manager in the league. If you are not the manager, you are at risk, I think. As the boss, you make the decisions and have then to stand by them. I didn't want it any other way. I had left a full-time job in Norway to come to Cardiff and was confident in doing a good job there. I had to be careful upon arriving as youth team coach as to how I was perceived. I knew that I could come up with the goods; I was confident of that so long as I had the backing. As a manager I had to be professional and be tough on people when required: I'd been there and seen and done it as a player all before. I believed that if I am the manger the decisions I make are mine alone and if I am proved wrong, I'm wrong. I will live by it.

When I first became a manager I wanted to win my practice matches, my friendly games, leagues and all. Players can see in you how much you want to win and if they can take this on board themselves, then you are on your way to getting a decent team together with good characters. This I feel was validated when as a boss I used to try and watch games every night, all across the country, it didn't matter. The players I signed may not have always been skillful but I wanted lads that were disciplined; winning or losing they must exert the same amount of effort. At Cardiff I signed players with ability and character who soon became favourites with the Ninian Park faithful. Boys like Nathan Blake, Stant, Carl Dale and Nick Richards. The latter came up from non-league football, just like myself.

I feel that in writing this book, I must give my Cardiff City players of the 1992/93 season a special mention individually. And as already detailed, the side won promotion as division champions and took the Welsh Cup in what was a memorable season for us all. So let's remember back in the day when I used to have the club play the Tina Turner track 'Simply the Best' as the players ran out on to the Ninian Park pitch to the roar of the crowd.

1 Gavin Ward

He was a very fit player, 6' 3" and not a bit of fat on him. His goal kicks often reached deep in to the opponent's half ala Ron Healey, a past City keeper in the mid-1970s.

2 Robbie James

You could put him anywhere in your team and he would do a great job. As previously stated in the Swansea chapter, I had the pleasure of playing with him at the Vetch when he was a nineteen-year-old. You could see then what potential he had. I miss him.

3 Jason Perry

Known fondly to the City supporter as 'Psycho' to win a game he would kick his granny. Jason was a 100% dedicated player who loved playing for Cardiff City FC.

4 Kevin Ratcliffe

I brought Kevin to south Wales after learning that he was to be released by his then-present club, Everton. He turned out to be one of my best signings; a great organiser at the back who always encouraged my young defenders around and about him. He proved a big boost to the dressing room and he soon became one of the lads immediately after I introduced him to the squad. I know Jason Perry was especially complimentary of him.

5 Damon Searle

A consistent defender with a good left foot. He never stopped talking on the pitch and loved to get forward and put in a decent cross. As a young lad, he made his way through the ranks at City via a Youth Training Scheme. For the 1992/93 season Damon played in every one of the forty two league games as well as all the various cup engagements. He works for the club today at their new Cardiff City stadium.

6 Cohen Griffith

He came to Cardiff as a striker but I switched him to play wide on the right-side of midfield. Cohen did an excellent job working up and down the right flank. He was fast and gave the team his all in every game. Spent six years at Cardiff and experienced promotion and relegation whilst at the club.

7 Nick Richardson

"Oh Nicky, Nicky, Nicky, Nicky, Nicky, Nicky Richardson..." I signed him from Halifax Town for £30,000 in August 1992 after being impressed by him after I attended a game there. A workman-like player with total commitment.

8 Paul Ramsey

I have already included a great deal about Paul and have always been impressed with his will to win. When I got him to sign for the club, it was the best piece of business I did whilst at City. As stated previously, Paul was like my right arm on the pitch.

9 Paul Millar

I was persuaded to sign him from Port Vale for £60,000 after seeing him smash in a hat-trick in the summer of 1991. A Belfast lad, 'Windy' as his team mates called him was an aggressive player, all left foot and a great professional. He had this habit of putting his arms up in the air prior to putting in a corner which the City fans used to copy! Paul hit some memorable goals for me especially including a forty yard smasher against Aldershot in one Friday night away match. Another came at the old Vetch ground in Swansea too. The fans also loved his belter at Doncaster which he relished as much as them by slapping their hands in celebration.

10 Nathan Blake

He had everything but belief in his own ability. Nathan was a fantastic athlete who was a big favourite at Cardiff City. I disagreed when he was sold to Sheffield United for £100,000. Should have had more games in a Wales shirt in my opinion but is remembered for a brilliant header scored in red.

11 Carl Dale

I went to watch Carl play after a recommendation from a friend in Wrexham. He subsequently became one of Cardiff's favourite sons. Two great feet. Carl struck the final brace of goals at Ninian Park in a charity match staged at the old ground shortly before the new stadium was ready for occupation. I was there that day too on the bench for one last time in a benefit game arranged for the Bobath Cymru charity (info@bobathwales.org) in Wales. Carl scored a penalty that day which he had done professionally for me in a number of games previously. By May 2009, this native North Wallian was back working as an electrician in Mansfield, a trade he was involved in prior to becoming a footballer.

12 Chris Pike

'Pikey' as he was called would drive me to fury! Sometimes I would be tearing my hair out whilst at others he would be outstanding for me. Carl had a great physique for a 6'3" striker and was very quick. He always seemed to play better in away games as the Ninian Park crowd seemed to get frustrated with him.

13 Phil Stant

"Who needs Cantona when we've got Stantona!" That was a City chant said to have originated at an away game at Northampton, which we won 1-2. Phil will tell you that at first he was embarrassed to be compared with the French genius Eric Cantona, then a Man United star, but he eventually became very proud of what the fans thought about him. 'Stanty' was stationed at Hereford as an Army bomb disposal man and this is where I first saw him play in their football team. He turned professional with them in 1986 and was an all-action player who loved to score goals in training or matches. As a professional, he had the knack of scoring on his various debuts and did so in a Cardiff City shirt against one of his former clubs, Hereford United. Not the easiest player to handle, after every game he would come to me and ask if he could come back down to Cardiff on Tuesdays (as he lived away) because I used to give my players the Monday off. I arranged for him to train at Mansfield every Tuesday and would ring them to check that he was there: he always was. I know that he respected me for that and we got on well. Writing in his enjoyable autobiography (Ooh Ah Stantona, From the Falklands to Europe - The story of a mothballing warrior, John Blake, 2006) he wrote: "Eddie was really old school and an autocratic guy. But his technique appealed to the Army lad in me, as I always prefer to know where I stand with people and there was no mistaking the fact that you certainly knew what Eddie thought of you!" Phil was a great goal scorer at whatever club he was playing for.

14 Lee Baddeley

I gave him his league debut as a nineteen year-old and he went on to play regularly in the first team. Kevin Ratcliffe, a fellow defender for me, nursed Lee through brilliantly. Lee was a former Youth Training Scheme lad and presented himself as a brave, whole-hearted player.

15 Derek Brazil

He was on loan at Swansea City from Manchester United when I saw him play for the first time. He struck me as a player that you could put into defence or midfield and he would do a decent job for you. I spoke to Alex Ferguson about him and he said that his loan period with the Swans was coming to an end, so I grabbed him. A Dublin-born defender who ran out in a City shirt across one hundred and forty one appearances during the 1992-95 period. I signed Derek for 40k and he turned out to be a very versatile footballer for the club. Getting a drink from him was like trying to draw blood from a stone; I think he had very deep pockets! A good professional and deep thinker about the game. He stayed in the football environment after retiring as a player, becoming the Haverford West manager in October 2006.

A LITTLE EXTRA

I thought it might be fun to include some comments about myself and the team from fans who were there throughout the double-winning season and who remember the celebrated team from the period. The comments are succinct and really sum up the time for me too.

"I loved this era. The dug-out in front of the Bob Bank when Eddie would walk towards us to a few thousand chanting "What's his name? Eddie, Eddie, Eddie May!" Players Carl Dale and Chris Pike terrorised up front...then the legend that is Phil Stant stepped in...we had Ramsey, Gibbins, Blake, Cohen, Robbie James, Nicky Richardson, Adams, Bird Jason Perry, Damon Searle, Derek Brazil....too many to name. Good times."

"That was when I pretty much first started taking an interest in Cardiff and he was a real figure. I'll never forget the fans singing "Eddie May's barmy army!" I thought that was the original 'barmy army' chant." (I seem to have had such things follow me throughout my career, what with this and another one at Wrexham back in my playing days. Even in 2010, when attending a centenary celebration for Cardiff City, I was greeted by the Eddie May 'Barmy Army' chant!

"I loved them, as I felt our fans were fantastic during those years, 1,500 City supporters off to Colchester and Northampton on Friday nights (and winning both times). That season, you felt we were going to win every game. The football for that level was superb."

"He was a hero to me: loved the Eddie May's barmy army chant."

"I remember the open Grange End packed out and the surges forward when we scored."

"Eddie will always be a City legend and nearly everyone who supported City then will name his as their all time favourite manager. He got the very best (and a bit more) out of the players who played for him: how many players left City and never went on to bigger things? Our away support was fantastic and worshiped the guy, the belief in everyone around the club was amazing and most of that arguably would be down to the manager."

DO THE AYATOLLAH

Welsh football fans are as vociferous as those at any club and at Cardiff the fans created many chants for their favourite players and I had one too. "Eddie May's Barmy Army" was a true original and when I returned to Ninian Park as a guest in 2009, a little while before they moved to the new Cardiff City stadium, the fans repeated it, much to my delight! It was a fantastic compliment.

The supporters were good to me, no doubt about it. Phil, Carl and Blakey all had their own chants too.

On the Bob Bank and Grange End sections of Ninian Park the die hard City fans once haunted much of the space. And a truly bizarre sight had to be when thousands of supporters did what they called the 'Ayatollah'.

This originated when I was manager there and the craze caught on and continues to be a familiar sight, to this day at the new stadium. The Ninian Park ground has gone and in its place is a housing estate but the tradition continues. To the uninitiated, what they do is ask you to 'do the Ayatollah' which is done by simply patting the top of the head with both hands flat.

I remember the first occasion when they asked me to do it (City fans always chant for others in different parts of the ground to do the motion) and I had no idea what they were on about! Some of our players had been requested to do it too and they were originally equally baffled.

Former City players and favoured visitors are requested to do the gesture too. When he was Sunderland manager, even the mighty Roy Keane did it once. I think that the craze began in 1990 and came about as a result of some City fans having attended a music gig that same year where the lead singer was doing something similar. It caught on and was introduced doggedly on the terraces. In addition, some fans back then would dress up in Middle Eastern garments to support, if that's the right word, its true origins. This stemmed from the distressed public mourners at the funeral of Ayatollah Khomeni also in the same year, which had been seen on television by the singer at the Cardiff gig and somehow incorporated into the show.

Looking on the internet, it has been noted that City fans first did their 'Ayatollah' at an away game at Lincoln City in September 1990 but the Scunthorpe game has also been noted.

8
TORQUAY, IRISH EDDIE
& BACK TO ENGLAND WITH BRENTFORD

Having left Cardiff City at the close of the 1994/95 season I was subsequently interviewed by the Torquay United chairman Michael Bateson at a time when his club was rooted to the bottom of the league. After chatting with him, I made a point of watching the team play two or three times and so I knew exactly how bad they were before Michael offered me the job as manager. I considered it an interesting challenge, initially. By the time of becoming their new boss in November 1995, the team had recorded a solitary win in their Endsleigh League Division Three campaign with a total of ten points collected.

Torquay might well be a beautiful part of the country but at the football club, lack of funds meant that it was a struggle for me from the start and it proved to be one of the toughest jobs, psychologically-speaking, that I had in my career. They were fighting for their survival with relegation meaning dropping out of the English league.

The gates at Plainmoor were not very big and a reminder of my recent past came calling via a domestic encounter with Cardiff City, at home, in February '96, resulting in a 0-0 draw. Kenny Hibbitt, then the latest manager at Cardiff, had his feathers ruffled by my appearance at Ninian Park in January '96 when I went to see their fixture with Leyton Orient. It was goal-less but I had gone along as I wanted to watch Orient, as they were our own next opponents. Hibbitt, a former Wolves player, was reported in the Welsh press that in his opinion, I should have stayed away from the ground. I disagreed and received a warm welcome from the home fans who remembered me for what I had achieved with them before. Hibbitt had arrived soon after I had left City following the new consortium taking control of Cardiff in 1994. Whatever, when we met Orient in late-January, we beat them 2-1 at our place.

"If it's not exactly 'Mission Impossible', it is the next best thing." Summarized Bateson shortly after I took on the post there. When you get offered a job like the one here, you always go into it thinking that you can bring the club success. This is the only way to think. You work hard as a manger and behind-the-scenes but for so many different reasons; it doesn't always go your way. I brought my old Leicester player Paul Ramsey in on loan and also tried to bolster the squad with Phil Stant but alas his then-club, Bury, wanted too much money for him. Paul, you might recall, had been my captain at Cardiff City too, and he was a great leader for me out on the pitch. In all, at Leicester he had played more than three hundred games for them before I brought him to Cardiff in 1991 for £100,000. Paul remembers his brief time at United well, "With Eddie as the manager, I enjoyed it there but we had a poor season with lots of injuries. I was at St Johnstone, in Scotland, and the standard of football there was poor so a move back into the English League was a big plus for me. I think I was there for about three months on loan. I had already experienced turmoil at Leicester in the latter part of my career so I could handle things at Torquay. I could cope with the changes as it was all experience." Digressing to life at Cardiff City, Paul saw a new side to that particular club. "When Terry Yorath came in as interim manager there, I felt that when I was asking him things about the club he wasn't giving the answer that I believed.

He was a nice enough man but I don't think he knew what was going on." On a lighter note, our professional relationship was always strong. "I liked Eddie a lot and always believed what he said to me," adds Paul, who nowadays is involved with the Leicester Legends, which arranges reunions for various fund-raising events. "He would never buy a drink but...." laughs the former Irish defender. It was not the last time that we would work together. When I worked briefly over in Finland with a club called Finn Pa, I learnt that Paul was playing in the country too. "After leaving Torquay and St Johnstone I played at a number of non-league clubs, many with former pros there." continues my former City captain. "I also moved to Finland and enjoyed playing for a club called KPV prior to getting a phone call from Eddie asking me to contact him as he had just arrived and taken charge at Finn Pa, then based in Helsinki. I eventually signed for them for a month or so but never played for them." Finn Pa or to give them their full title, Finnairin Palloilijjatt, was a Helsinki-based club that enjoyed six seasons in the top level of domestic football. They went on to finish the 1997 season in third spot before a brutal blow of relegation and lack of financial support eventually saw them fold.

Returning to the end of that catastrophic season at Torquay, we finished bottom of the table having accredited four further wins and eleven draws since I took over. Points gathered came from Orient, Fulham and Darlington with draws scrapped over against the likes of Scarborough, Exeter City, Gillingham, Hereford and Chester City.

Fortunately for Torquay United, Stevenage Borough, champions of the Conference League below us that season, failed to meet the necessary safety criteria for their ground to be used in the higher division and therefore United retained their League status. Mr Bateson, often barracked by the fans, sold the club in 2007 some seventeen years since he first got involved there.

My first foray into football away from either England or Wales came in the appealing form of Dundalk FC over in Ireland in March 1997. I met with their chairman, a delightful character called Enda McGuill, after a recommendation from a Daily Mirror reporter in the area, Robert Reid. The latter was a massive Cardiff fan and we had gotten to know each other quite well when the Irish job was made available. Robert used to watch the Bluebirds whenever he could and would stay at the Cardiff guest house owned by my former partner Marlene.

Dundalk is on the border of southern Ireland and the north and the team had a good following led by a charismatic chairman. I went over to see the set-up and agreed to take charge for the pre-season in readiness for the opening of the 1997/98 Premier division campaign. The standard of football over there in the League of Ireland surprised me a bit as it was quite good. In all, I managed the team for ten games before an offer came along which I simply could not refuse.

All the time that I was there, I still had the inkling to return to the English League. I had left Cardiff because they had wanted to bring in their own man which happens in football all the time but I wanted to try again. People often get the sack in the game in spite of doing a good job. Frequently, the powers-that-be at any given club want to be able to manipulate you by telling you what to do but I'm not that kind of personality. I did my own job and that was it. I would listen to directors but they never told me what to do. At Dundalk with the 'Lilywhites', Enda made everybody welcome and during my period in charge, he was pleased enough with the performance of his side on the pitch. It was then that I got a telephone call from David Webb, an ex-player who many years before had won the F.A. Cup with Chelsea and who was now chairman at Division Two side Brentford.

We had known each other whilst at Leicester City in the late-1970s during which time he would occasionally play for us in the reserves, in the highly-respected Football Combination league. He was jovial pro and we had got on well back then. So when he offered me the job as manager with him, I took it and left Dundalk.

It was my good fortune to be back in London, as Brentford was situated in the borough of Hounslow. The problem was, as an ex-player, when David took charge as chairman, he wanted to rule the roost. Even though he had me as the manager and I had been a pro myself, he still wanted to pick the team. I had to tell him that I had not come to Griffin Park to be a patsy for him. I had a job to do and I had to do it, not him. Sometimes you come across a chairman who has had a football background; they think that they can over-rule, especially if things are going wrong on the pitch. They can have a tendency to start telling you what to do: they want to select the team and ask why so-and-so isn't in the side or why another has been selected. It does get very difficult. My relationship with David was heated at times.

After about six or so months with the Bees, I said to him, "This isn't working." When I had attempted to bring in new faces, he often disagreed and the whole thing became untenable. For me, I wasn't enjoying the football there and within the confines of such an environment, I felt that I had to step aside even though it was a job in English football that I was walking away from. Things culminated in a big row between us, partly based upon a player I wanted to sign which he had blocked. He told me there was no money and that I had to make do with things as they were. It just wasn't happening and I agreed to leave. I had no idea when I first got the job at Brentford just what it was going to be like there for me. I think that he should have thought more from a chairman's perspective. You cannot think as an ex-player, certain things are appropriate but he was too much in that he was doing things that he wanted me to then implement. By this point I had been in the game a long time and wasn't prepared to work under these circumstances. I left in the beginning of November 1997 and David took over for the remainder of the season. Sadly, the club was relegated. I think that I only brought in one player whilst I was there: Charlie Oatway from my former club, Cardiff City.

It was a tough time for the club on the pitch but we did manage some decent wins early on in the season; a 5-3 defeat of Shrewsbury Town in the League Cup was followed by two home wins against Grimsby Town, 3-1 and Gillingham, 2-0. There was not much else to smile about apart from a 3-0 home victory against Walsall in mid-October. We managed nine draws up until my departure but lost a dozen more against teams which included Watford, Southend United and Bristol City.

Previous names at Brentford before me had included former Spurs man Steve Perryman and David himself; managing the side between 1993 and 1997 when in August of that year, I came in, assisted by former Chelsea player Clive Walker. When I had first arrived there, all of their best players had been sold previously due to debt problems and the fans knew that the team was in risk of relegation. At the time of being interviewed for the post, I had been told that there would be money for new players but that proved to be untrue. I think being chairman at the club was David's first appointment and he obviously found it difficult. In certain areas you have to allow the manager to make decisions: he should not have tried to do everything himself. I made a big mistake by leaving Irish football because I was happy there.

But as I said, when the Brentford job came up, I was more than tempted to return.

David Webb was a tough-talking man who wanted to be manager and chairman. He had previously managed at my fledgling club where I had first signed professional terms as a player, Southend United and had also been in the managerial seat at Griffin Park before I got there. Also at Chelsea, AFC Bournemouth and Torquay for short periods, David had ruffled feathers at the latter club where his tenure was not a success. Like me, he made his mark as a defender and had success as a centre forward when called upon to do so. In all, he made more than 500 appearances as a player. David had transferred to Leicester City in September 1977 and stayed there for a little over a year, making thirty three appearances when the great Jock Wallace was in charge. He had also been an amateur with my childhood favourite club, West Ham United.

At the point of my departure from Brentford, following twenty or so matches, I said to him, "I don't want to be here and you don't want me here." I think that he expected the team to be up there competing high in the league. Coincidentally, the Brentford club song is the Beatles favourite, Hey Jude. A tune also utilised by Cardiff City in recent times. And continuing the theme, the former's record victory was a 9-0 thrashing of Wrexham but I hasten to add that this was back in the early-1960s before I got there as a player!

Big name managers who had reaped rewards as players can often struggle because of their own ability. They expect people to perform and do things like they did when playing. But a lot of footballers are not like that. If a lad has a certain skill, it is nice to see but you can only play to your own limitations. They expect a bit more than their players are capable of: no one could defend like Bobby Moore but he didn't stay long in the game after he had finished playing. I think he only managed at two clubs and that was it. I had Jock Wallace at Leicester and Arfon Griffiths had John Neal at Wrexham to learn from but there are many casualties in the game. You get frustrated.

Often a perspective other than your own is of value, and so I will include some comments from Brentford fans from when I was involved with their club. A fan known online as 'KGB', remembers my final match in charge; a 0-1 defeat at home to Carlisle. "One of the worst and most embarrassing memories for me as a Bees fan was watching Eddie walk down the touchline after his final match. We all knew he was going to be sacked; that he had been royally shafted and didn't deserve to have been put in that position." He adds, "Given better resources, he could have been a decent manager for us as he tried to entertain as much as possible. He slowed as he walked past the Paddock (the home fans area) and with a knowing smile said, "I know." The man showed so much class and dignity in that brief moment." Russell, another fan also commenting on the Brentford forum site Griffin Park was at the same match too, "Eddie trudged along the touchline and someone muttered something like 'That's not good enough" to which he replied, "I know but what can I do?" He knew that he was gone and the deed was done the following day. I have nothing but sympathy for him." I left the club on 5 November and by the close of that season in the following May, Brentford were relegated as were Southend.

A lot of people think that this club or that is not for them and easily dismiss a prospective job very quickly. But for me, it was a case of wanting to get back in to football. Sometimes you can make a wrong decision and I clearly did by moving to Brentford. When I left there, I had some correspondence from fans supporting my involvement with their club.

The thing is that you know that you are at a club to try to improve the situation; that you are there to do a job. But if someone interferes, you are going to struggle. If you try to develop the team, they often don't want to know. And they moan about the team not being good enough and question why the club isn't winning games. You reply that you need some decent players to do this. Nobody gets the sack in football for nothing, do they? If you go into a job then that club must be struggling. They do not change their manager because they are in the top five of the table usually. The team must be faltering. When you start in the post, all this very rapidly comes to the fore. You broach the subject with the chairman and inform him that the team isn't good enough and again, sometimes they do not want to know. It is obvious then to see why their previous manager got sacked or left.

My second involvement with Irish football, after keeping Dundalk from relegation subsequently took me to Drogheda United. They had just been promoted to the Premier division at the end of the 1998/99 season. Known as 'The Drogs', the team was a yo-yo club in the Irish league and were playing in the First Division when I joined them. They were a relatively new club, being founded in 1975 and based on the Irish east coast in an industrial port town.

At Dundalk, I had ten games to work with and managed to keep the club away from relegation but I didn't have such luck at United. I was brought in to start in December 1999, following the departure of the previous manager a short while earlier. The team was sitting at the bottom of the table and I was one in a long line of mangers to try to steer an already rocky ship. I became their first full-time gaffer in the following January when we held the then-leaders Shelborne United to a goal-less draw.

I set about my usual approach of bringing in some new faces and soon Ray Wallace (brother of Rod) and Chris Roberts, a former Cardiff City apprentice arrived. My chairman even wrote an open letter to a regional newspaper asking fans to be patient whilst we attempted to kick-start things. Unfortunately, Drogheda was not structured well enough to utilise having a full-time manager like myself in the job. Consequently, they decided to revert to being a semi-professional club and by the end of the season were bottom of the league. I left pretty soon after.

In the football world, you never know what the next opportunity might be and back in 1999 I knew a couple of football agents and asked them to put my name forward for consideration for a curious vacancy! It was for the national boss of Pakistan. I sent my CV and the Pakistan Football Association then invited me for an interview in London, where I met their representative. A deal was struck and I was to sign a 3-year contract but in October 1998, a political coup over there meant that it was unsafe for me to travel to Pakistan as there was much unrest with a conflict with India seemingly likely at the time.

It was whilst awaiting confirmation to travel out that I became involved with Drogheda. I went over there and worked in anticipation of the Pakistan people to clarify my employment in readiness for the 2002 World Cup qualifiers. The then-current Pakistan Prime Minister had been on a plane which had been refused permission to land by the Chief of the Army, who later took on the aforementioned role himself. They had to land elsewhere and there was a political coup in the country thereafter. I subsequently received a call from their Football Association representative who confirmed the problems and I said that I had been watching it unfold on the news over here. It was a couple of months before I was due to start work but it was clear that the unrest in the country would make it unsafe to go there. The situation dragged on and I then received a job offer to go to Ireland which I took in the meantime hoping that the Pakistan job would eventually come up.

Regrettably, the green light to start never came and I have always wondered at what might have been.

Following on from the Brentford job, across the 1999/00 season I found that people working in the game would ring me up to ask me to scout for them. I enjoyed doing this when not involved with a club in a coaching capacity. The way scouting worked was that you would go to see a team that a particular club was soon due to meet, define their formation, and observe how they played, note their best players and possible weaknesses and write it all up in a report. One job saw me working for my old Chicago Sting team mate Ian Story Moore.

I think that he is still in the game now and was recently involved with Aston Villa (another club I scouted for). Another boss I worked for was Frank Burrows, then in charge of Swansea City. He was an old fashioned defender and as Cardiff City manager from 1986 won a promotion and two Welsh Cups up until his departure in 1989. He was Swansea boss for four years from 1991 onwards assisted by former Wrexham player Bobbie Smith, whose job as youth team coach I took over at Cardiff City.

The way things work in football is that people get to know whether or not you are working and often put a bit of work your way if it's the latter. I got a great buzz from doing this kind of job as I would be mingling again with lots of football people. At half time, you could go in and have a cup of tea and socialise. Lots of us would share information about players and job vacancies so it was a useful way of networking. Some would leave immediately after the final whistle, but I would hang about and see who was there and chat. I applied for two or three prospective coaching/ managerial vacancies at the time but was happy to be involved with the game in any way I could until another job came my way. Another did subsequently surface but in a form of which I could not have imagined: Africa.

Above: Winning the FA Cup in Malwai, 2005 and the Premier League title with Highlanders in Zimbabwe. In all, my time spent working abroad was the most satisfying of my career.

9
AFRICA EDDIE

In that complex continent that is Africa, there is always somebody monitoring the media and I felt that I needed to be winning things and spread the word to keep my name in the spotlight for prospective new jobs. I think that I did this as I was to become involved with a number of clubs across the continent there.

My initial foray into African football was not all that exciting but my time there ultimately proved to be a very rewarding experience. Former Wimbledon player John Fashanu was an ambassador for African football around 2000, which was when I spoke with him about a possible vacancy with a league club (he was also involved with Welsh league side Barry Town FC after I had moved on). John put my name forward for a vacancy at South African side Bush Bucks. Founded 1957, the team played in the East London Stadium in Port Elizabeth until folding in 2006. They were to rise again by 2007 but in the form of Lion City FC. I wasn't there for very long as problems with my visa ultimately prohibited my employment in the country even though I had been working with the team in the meantime. There haven't been many jobs that I have not enjoyed but this was probably one of them. I had a confrontation with the assistant manager there, Ngubane, from whom I did not feel I was getting enough support. He had recently been moved up and clearly wanted the managerial post for himself whilst the club was looking around for a new boss. We argued quite a lot and the players were tending to back him more than me so I decided to move on.

Bush Bucks are a Premier League side and had a decent team when I worked there. This was where I got my first taste of African football. I picked up things very quickly about how they worked; I could see that when players had the ball, they tended to forget about what was going on around them. Trying to suggest to them about running off the ball went down badly as they believed that they were running for nothing. That was their mentality. I attempted to drum it into them that if somebody has possession, he has to have one or two options with team mates moving off the ball. It was things like this that I tried to implement. The players were very skillful but what they lacked was organisation and discipline. By the end of the year, I moved on to Uganda, with a team known as 'Express'. I got that job thanks to a reporter who was also working as a scout in the game. Not a great deal occurred here until I got a subsequent phone call from the chairman of a Zimbabwe-based club called Highlanders. His name was Kenny Ndebele and we still talk on the phone today. It was to be from here that success in Africa really did explode for me. Kenny left the club in 2010, some nine years after I arrived at the club as Head Coach in 2001 and he later advanced to become the Premier Soccer League Secretary General.

Express are Uganda's oldest established football club, who play in the Super League there which was created in 1968 and consists of 18 teams. The club has won the league title a half-dozen times and are known as the 'Red Eagles' or more succinctly, 'FC'. And in case you wondered, the football club originated with links to Uganda Express Newspapers: hence the name. Based in the Kampala area, FC has vociferous support from across the country and is the best supported team there.

What I learnt from being in Africa is that the mentality is different in each country and they have clear distinctions between them. I found that from my experience, I got used to dealing with a lot of undisciplined players in Uganda particularly. Some would not attend training yet still demand that they play in the team. I think English coaches like myself got regarded as being too tough, too strong. It is because they tried to get away with things such as missing training. All these aspects are the African mentality and I mean that in the nicest possible way.

From my arrival in Zimbabwe, I loved my whole career there: not just with Highlanders either. There were decent grounds, often situated in the national stadium where two teams would be based in the same city. One would play on the Saturday, whilst the other would follow on the Sunday. Highlanders played in the Bulawayo region and have fanatical fans following the fortunes of the club. The Africans in general are mad about their football. I was appointed in July 2001 and we won the Castle Lager Premier Soccer League title after a goal-less meeting with the Black Rhinos in early-October 2002. At the time, we had taken sixty points from twenty six matches, which meant that we could not be caught by anyone in the league. Our home ground was the Barbourfields Stadium with the team playing in their black and white colours. We got gates of 30,000 and it was the African equivalent of Liverpool. It was all about tradition at Highlanders. Their domestic league is also known as CBZ Premier Soccer League due to sponsorship tie-ins and is the top league in the country. It was created in 1980. Highlanders are the biggest club in Bulawayo, the second biggest city in the country.

The endearing thing about Africa is that on every patch of waste ground, you see children playing football. I had a good time whilst I was there as I had arrived not knowing what I was going to meet or what was likely to transpire. The Africans are fantastic people in my eyes.

In some African countries you would get definable seasons. Not many but their winter was still fairly warm to someone like me. During my initial year there, I lived in a hotel and subsequently a bungalow around the hotel grounds: I was well taken care of. Success on the field also saw me being awarded Coach of the year for that first season. When I would walk along the street, people would recognize me from the football club and were very warm towards me. Behind the scenes, clubs took their sport seriously and pitches were well-kept and the whole thing was well organised. Everything had a structure and ran smoothly. My players at 'Bosso' (as Highlanders are known) were mostly Zimbabwe-born but we did have a couple of South Africans. I found that I had to be cautious in mixing fellow Africans as sometimes there could be friction between them. Some of us will remember Zimbabwe from the days when it was called Rhodesia.

My club captain was a guy called Dezzy Kapenya, a twenty-nine-year-old defender who, along with a midfielder called Ngodzo, were two of our star players.

Things ran smoothly for me and I hardly had a problem at all because the club was proving successful. I controlled the whole thing there, from coaching and training methods and more. I had assistants working with me and they appreciated my methods. I taught them certain things that they had not heard of such as the importance of a good warm-up before a match. Also, the value of stretching exercises. They never used to incorporate such things before me and they welcomed my knowledge.

Further trophies followed: the Independence (FA) Cup also 2001 and a repeat of the 'double' in 2002 (League and Cup). Highlanders were the equivalent of Manchester United in Zimbabwe. When I eventually moved on, someone asked me why the club failed to build on their winning ways. I replied, "Because I wasn't there!" The achievements we made were continuous but I realised when I first arrived that I was again on trial. I told them that success would come but it would take time to develop. But it arrived much sooner than I anticipated. During training I would stop them and say to a player, "If you get the ball, then others have to make runs in such-and-such a place." They freely absorbed all this and listened to my advice. That's what I liked about them: they were enthusiastic and quite prepared to implement my methods.

It was whilst with Highlanders that I was made an offer from Black Leopards, a South African Premiership side. I was flattered by their interest but the news proved unsettling to both myself and the club.

I decided to stay in Zimbabwe as I was happy with things there. However, people at Highlanders seemed to think that I was about to leave and the press would often report that I was about to depart too. Another time, I had an offer for a job elsewhere but I could not reassure my present employers that I wanted to stay with them. It was all speculation and what's known as 'paper talk'. The Africans have an insatiable appetite for football-related news and so I was often dragged into things. Highlanders thought that I was speaking to other clubs behind their backs even though I was most definitely not. Being successful it was obvious that speculation would link you with other clubs and it happens in the UK all the time, doesn't it. Established in 1926, some past players that have played for Highlanders include ex-Liverpool 'keeper Bruce Grobelaar and Peter N'dlovu.

I was to take up the lucrative offer made by Amazulu FC, another club in the Zimbabwe Premier League, and moved there for the 2003/04 season. I didn't have to travel very far, as they also played in Bulawayo; in the same stadium too. I was nervous about the response from the Highlanders followers when we met them in a local derby. We beat them but things were okay. The chairman at Amazulu was a very rich man who made me an offer that was too tempting to turn down. Regrettably, he wanted to choose the team himself and this was a new problem for me as at Highlanders things were very different. We won the Championship in 2001 and the chairman offered lots of things but nothing came from them.

In Zimbabwe, there are 3 or 4 teams which vie for the title of the best side, with Amazulu being one of them. Their rivalry with Highlanders is the local equivalent of Welsh sides Cardiff City and Swansea City. Things at Amazulu were not as easy for me as at Highlanders because of the concerns I had with my chairman there. He ran the club independently and made all the decisions himself, there was no committee to debate anything. If I wanted anything implemented, I had to talk just with him. I think a similar set up is with Abramovich at Chelsea. It is not the healthiest way to run a club. One man cannot always be right. Look how many managers Chelsea have had and this is clearly proven. You cannot run a football club like this but money talks and there is not much you can do about it. Chelsea's revenue for 2010-11 totalled £225.6m.

From Zimbabwe, I moved to Malawi to become the new Head Coach of MTL FC. They are one of the two biggest teams in the country and it was not a great distance for me to move there, geographically-speaking.

Football in Africa is different in that they love their football there. People come in and take over a club and use it to promote their own businesses. MTL was a well-run club and up there on a par with their neighbours at Highlanders.

Twynne Pirre, presently the President of the league in Zimbabwe, and previously the chairman at Caps United had asked me to go there when I left the job at Highlanders. He knew the chairman of MTL was looking for a coach and I got a recommendation. A deal was struck and in 2005 we won the national FA Cup and the club was runners-up in the domestic league. There was not much difference between these clubs as they were both football daft and craved success. MTL Wanderers are also known as 'Nomads' and that November Malawi Cup win came after extra-time and penalties against Admarc Tigers. We won the trophy by a 5-4 score line. At MTL, we had a good base of youngsters who performed well.

The Malawi people proved to be very warm and I got recognised everywhere I went. MTL was a club that demonstrated tremendous hospitality towards me and had well-disciplined players; probably the best I ever dealt with. Prior to taking the job there I had canvassed the views of a guy that I knew from my Cardiff days. I rang him and he said that if I got offered a post over there that I should definitely take it. There was a lot of British business activity there and a heavy industrial influence from China.

Money influenced my next move across Africa; this time to take on the coaching role at Power Dynamos in Kitwe, Zambia. It was by now 2006 but with hindsight, I have to accept that this was a bad move for me. I made a big mistake in switching to Zambia. My season there was okay, we finished in third position and the club was happy with the way that we had performed on the pitch. The style of football in Zambia could be recognized as being very English-like; with more long balls proving common. I did enjoy it there but found it more difficult to fit in. And again, they too had fanatical fans. I would say that I did have problems with the internal set-up at Dynamos, as it was hard to get things changed. As a new coach, you have ideas and want to implement them as soon as possible but at this club, they didn't like change. It was a case of getting the job done but deep down, I was not really enjoying it.

Players there were much bigger and the domestic game is far more noticeably physical than in other African nations. As a club, Power Dynamos was a big one. They had their own training ground facility and a city-based stadium to play in situated in the south of the country.

By 2008, I had been out of the game since leaving Power Dynamos in 2006 but a job as Technical Director with the South African side Black Leopards brought me back into the game. You may recall that I had previously been offered a post with them back when I was at Highlanders but had declined their offer. On this occasion, an agent called Benji made all the running as he dealt with the chairman at Leopards, a man called David Tedelia. David was another of those success-driven business people.

The club already had a young coach and I came in as the new Technical Director, a post that was a new experience for me. The team had not enjoyed a good season immediately before I arrived and so there was scope for improvement. They realised that the coach, a former player called Joel, would need an experienced hand to help out. It was pre-season when I had expressed my interest in the vacancy and things went alright there and I felt that the standard of football was very high. I advised Joel and would say to him that he should give the team talk at half-time and I would add my comments too. This attitude was well-received by the chairman and I knew that I was there to offer my professional opinion and help guide the coach and players only; I wasn't after anybody's job. I did say to the players during their first game that I wanted to see what they could do; that they should show me what they could offer the club. This was an away game at Johannesburg that ended in a draw. I was satisfied with the new role and got the opportunity, via training, to introduce some shooting or crossing practice or whatever I thought necessary. I made sure that the players viewed the introduction of such ideas as coming from Joel. Not long after, in April 2009, events back home in the UK with Marlene's family meant that my time in Africa was finally coming to a close.

My record and name abroad is a good one and I continue to monitor events away from home. Sometimes clubs in Africa get put off before even considering British coaches for possible vacancies as they think you will want too high a salary. In Africa, they dance all day and all night when success comes to their clubs. Professionally, I have had more peace of mind working abroad then I have in the UK.

JOBS THAT GOT AWAY

Often in football, there are two or three jobs which just do not work out. You get offered the post and think that you are going to get the opportunity to make a mark but as you know by now, sometimes you don't get given the time for that to happen. Financial concerns at a club create an instability which effects the coach and playing staff directly.

After being a player at both Wrexham and Swansea and experiencing the highs and lows of management with Cardiff, I suppose it was inevitable that I would find my way to Newport County FC at some point. Like a number of players, many find themselves playing for one, two or three of the Welsh clubs but David Giles had played at all four when they had full league status (Newport are now in the Blue Square Bet Conference, the same league as Wrexham and other former Football League names such as Grimsby Town, Mansfield, York City) and here I was in July 1988 at their Somerton Park ground, the old home of the Ironsides?

County had achieved tremendous success when my old Qatar and Cardiff City mate Len Ashurst managed them in the late-1970s and in to the early-1980s. But, by the time I arrived there after working in Iceland, they had lost their league status and now found themselves in the Conference. County were a club with a league set-up and although losing their league status was a disaster for them, their infrastructure was that of a league standard, so I was tempted to return.

I came in as a replacement for Brian Eastwick, a guy who had taken over my coaching role at Leicester previously. At the time of accepting a two year contract with Newport, I had left my appointment in Iceland with KS after six games as I had an agreement with the chairman there that if a club in the UK came in for me I would be allowed to leave. I spoke with Lincoln's Colin Murphy, as his club had been relegated from the Football League but managed to claw their way back after a season away. I picked his brains as to how we could do this for County but all the while there were stirrings of a projected takeover at Somerton Park which had been denied at the time of my arrival. Back in 1988 I was involved for a short period at Lincoln with Colin there as manager. He used to come and watch Leicester City play when I was youth team coach there and consequently, we became good friends. He was looking for an assistant and I helped out.

I brought in former Wales and Swansea City player John Mahoney as my new assistant at Newport. 'Josh' as he was known, was a cousin of John Toshack, and had himself applied for the vacant managerial post at County before I was offered it. Another ex-Cardiff player, John Lewis, had before me endured a brief spell as player-manager but couldn't prevent the club from being relegated. Continuing my association with Josh, he had been signed by my former Southend and Wrexham team mate/ and manager respectively, John Neal during his playing days at Middlesbrough (when the latter was manager there).

New faces purported to buy the club but it soon became clear that they could not raise the necessary money and things collapsed. I was made aware of the financial distress at the club when one day, a removal van appeared at Somerton Park to take away the office furniture. What a disaster this period was for me, I only lasted a month there but my record at County was supreme: we never lost a game because we never actually played any! Such drama happens in football, alas.

11
REFLECTIONS

In the summer of 2009, the powers-that-be at Cardiff City rang me to offer the opportunity of putting together a team to meet my former Charlton colleague Lennie Lawrence in the inaugural match at the new Cardiff City Stadium. I think that the club wanted to utilize two former managers that had achieved success for them in the past to launch their future in the new stadium. I was honoured to be asked to do it and the event brought back some great memories for me and I enjoyed it as it was flattering to see that they thought so much of me. I didn't hesitate to return as my original departure from Cardiff City, when they were based at the neighbouring Ninian Park, now sadly demolished, was not in my hands. It was different people wanting to bring in their own man so I was okay with getting involved once more.

The match was staged at the new stadium on 4th July with my team included the likes of the excellent Jason Perry and Nathan Blake whilst Carl Dale, Cohen Griffiths and Derek Brazil turned out for Lennie's squad. I recently leant that my old captain Paul Ramsey was disappointed not to be asked to play that day but knowing of his recent knee problems perhaps he might not have been able to? Graham Kavanagh, a more recent Bluebird, and a very popular one with the fans, played for Lennie's side. I think he did this because 'LL' had given him his league debut at Middlesbrough previously.

I had sat in the old dug-out at Ninian Park one last time for a charity match game that featured a number of former City names including many of those that turned out for the subsequent 'Allstars' match at the new stadium. It was in aid of Bobath Cymru and was good to say farewell to the place whilst also raising funds for the Welsh charity.

Everybody was pleased when the new stadium was built and obviously the club has the Premiership in its sights. The stadium is beautiful but the team has to do it on the pitch. What happens when a new owner or investor arrives is they do their research into the quality of the club and what crowds they get before any investment occurs. But the thing is that they don't like failure so the pressure for instant success is immense. A lot of people liked the Vetch Field and didn't want to leave it but like Ninian Park, it was an old stadium. Ninian had one social room for use after the game and now at the new stadium they have two or three different options which proved popular.

You can have a meal before or after the match. There are no floodlight pylons like they had at the old ground and the modern stadium has changed dramatically. Many speak fondly about Ninian Park or the Vetch but it is important as a football club that you do not stand still.

Summing up is a pleasant thing to do as it brings back so many nice memories. In my early days, money never came into things: it was simply that I wanted to play football and when the opportunity came to be a professional, it was a god-send for me. Of course there are certain things I wish I could change; some that I regret and some things that happened to me which I could never have imagined.

When I was playing, I was content: I was happy. Starting out at Southend United, which wasn't far from my home and the man who signed me was a former boss from my favourite club, West Ham, was tremendously fortunate for me.

I don't regret anything from my playing days at all.

If anything, these came afterward and I include the following. In the Sunday papers there were stories linking my name with Everton and Bolton but as a player you are not that concerned with such speculation as you just get on with your job of playing football. The Wrexham managerial job came up after a lot of media speculation about me being offered the post in 1985. But as I have already detailed, I tried to be a little too clever, in as much as I wanted the job so badly. In those days managers and coaches were being paid more than the players. I got a bit greedy and told them I needed to be earning something near to what I was getting as assistant manager with Charlton, who I was then working with in the Second Division. Wrexham was in the division immediately below them.

In recent years, being back in Wales after some time away and involved with African football, the drop down to working with local Welsh clubs like Porthcawl, Haverford West, Merthyr Tydfil and Llanelli was a pronounced one for me. They were vastly different in their financial structures from the clubs that I had previously worked with. At those mentioned above, I got involved because I knew the chairman there and did it simply to help them out. But I never looked upon it as just something I could do on the side, if I go somewhere; I have got to win things. Personally, I don't think it is a good idea if you come down to that level of football for very long. At the moment I am waiting to see if a job comes up but I won't go to another club at this recent level because I was not getting the response that I expected from players: the quality is just not there.

The financial restraints at these clubs make it impossible to bring in new players and so forth. Today, I continue to keep an eye on the results of most of my old clubs and I monitor world football too.

Looking back, I remember when we completed the 'double' at Cardiff and I was invited to attend a presentation at a Hilton hotel in London where Manchester United supremo Sir Alex Ferguson paid me a huge compliment,

"What you do as a manager is what real management is about," he said. "Because you don't have access to the amount of money that I have but you get the results."

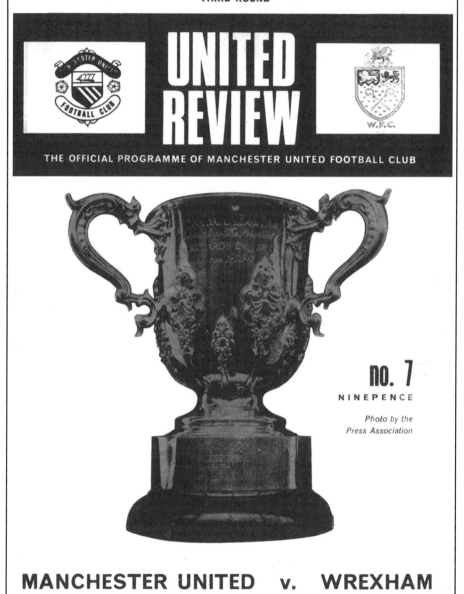

FOOTBALL LEAGUE CUP COMPETITION
THIRD ROUND

UNITED REVIEW

THE OFFICIAL PROGRAMME OF MANCHESTER UNITED FOOTBALL CLUB

no. 7

NINEPENCE

Photo by the Press Association

MANCHESTER UNITED v. WREXHAM

SEPTEMBER 23rd 1969   KICK-OFF 7-45 P.M.

The 1969/ 1970 season was full of adventure for Wrexham and saw us come face-to-face with the mighty United at Old Trafford for this League Cup meeting. I had a goal disallowed during the match which we lost 2-1.

STATISTICS

Wrexham

Promoted Division Three	1969 - 70
Welsh Cup	1971/ 72, 1974/ 75

Swansea City

Promoted to Division Three	1978 - 79

PLAYING STATS

Southend United

January 1965 - 1968, 117 appearances, 3 goals.

1964 - 65	Division 3/ 12th	W21	D9	L21
1965 - 66	Division 3/ 21st [R]	W19	D5	L28
1966 - 67	Division 4/ 6th	W22	D10	L17
1967/ 68	Division 4/ 6th	W21	D14	L14

Wrexham

June 1968 - 1976, 337 appearances, 35 goals

1968/ 69	Division 4/ 9th	W18	D21	L7
1969/ 70	Division 4/ 2nd	W26	D9	L11
1970/ 71	Division 3/ 9th	W18	D13	L15
1971/ 72	Division 3/ 16th	W16	D8	L22
1972/ 73	Division 3/ 12th	W14	D17	L15
1973/ 74	Division 3/ 4th	W22	D12	L12
1974/ 75	Division 3/ 13th	W15	D15	L16
1975/ 76	Division 3/ 6th	W20	D12	L14

Chicago Sting

1976 (summer loan) 18 appearances, 7 goals

Swansea City

| 1976/ 77 | Division 4/ 5th | W23 | D13 | L10 |
| 1977/ 78 | Division 4/ 3rd [P] | W23 | D10 | L13 |

Leicester City

| Bass Youth Cup winners | 1979 |
| Division Two champions | 1979 -1980 |

Gor Mahia

| Kenyan Championship | 1982 |

Tornado FC

Runners-up

| Norwegian Division Two | 1990 |

Cardiff City

Welsh Cup Winners	1992 & 1993
Division Three Champions	1993
Barclays Division Three Manager of Month	
(February and March)	1993

Highlanders FC

| Zimbabwe Independence Cup | 2001 |
| Premier League Championship | 2001 |

Zimbabwe Independence Cup	2002
Premier League Championship	2002

Amazulu FC

Premier League Championship	2003

MTL FC

Malawi FA Cup	2005
Runners-up Malawi League	2005

Leicester City	1978 - 1982
English Second Division	1978 - 1979: 17th
English Second Division	1979 - 1980: 1st [P]
English First Division	1980 - 1981: 21st [R]
English Second Division	1981 - 1982: 8th
Gor Mahia, Kenya	1982
Charlton Athletic	1983 -1986
English Second Division	1982- 1983: 17th
English Second Division	1983 - 1984: 13th
English Second Division	1984 - 1985: 17th
English Second Division	1985 - 1986: 2nd [P]
Al Nahada, Qatar	1986
KS Sigulford, Iceland	1987
Tornado FC, Norway	1989 -1990
Cardiff City	1990 - 1994
Barry Town	1994 - 1995
Torquay United	Nov 1995 - May 1996

Endsleigh Division Three	1995 - 1996: 21st
Dundalk, Ireland	1997
League of Ireland, Premier Division	
Brentford	1997
Nationwide Division Two	21st (left Nov 1997)
Drogheda	1999
League of Ireland, Premier Division	
Highlanders FC, Zimbabwe	2001 -2002
Amazulu FC, Zimbabwe	2003 - 2004
MTL FC, Malawi	2005
Power Dynamos, Zambia	2006 - 2007
Black Leopards, South Africa	2008